Servicemember's Guide to a College Degree

0 11557 03066 2

Servicemember's Guide to a College Degree

2nd Edition

Larry J. Anderson

STACKPOLE
BOOKS

Copyright © 2002 by Stackpole Books

Published by
Stackpole Books
5067 Ritter Road
Mechanicsburg, PA 17055-6921
www.stackpolebooks.com

Printed in the United States of America

10 9 8 7 6 5 4 3 2 1

Second Edition

Cover design by Wendy Reynolds
Photographs by Susanne Garvey Anderson

Library of Congress Cataloging-in-Publication Data

Anderson, Larry J., 1968–
    Servicemember's guide to a college degree / Larry J. Anderson.—2nd ed.
        p. cm.
    Rev. ed. of: Soldier's guide to a college degree. 1st ed. c1998.
    Includes bibliographical references and index.
    ISBN 0-8117-3066-2
    1. Soldiers—Education, Non-military—United States. 2. College credits—United States. 3. Degrees, Academic—United States. I. Anderson, Larry, 1968– Soldier's guide to a college degree. II. Title.
    U716 .A853 2002
    378.2'088355—dc21
                                                                    2002008768

Contents

APPENDICES

Preface

There are opportunities for all servicemembers to earn college credit, even without attending class. Servicemembers working on graveyard or rotating shifts, deploying overseas or to the field, or going on extended temporary duty can earn college credit. Many servicemembers mistakenly believe that college credit can be obtained only by sitting in a classroom during daytime hours as a professor lectures. Most servicemembers are unaware of the many nontraditional programs and opportunities.

There are several ways in which servicemembers can get college credits: from their military education and training; by examination in subjects for which they can get complete advanced study materials; through accredited colleges that have nontraditional education programs designed especially for military personnel; from Servicemembers Opportunity Colleges (SOC)—an extensive network of colleges that have coordinated programs among themselves, which are designed to accommodate a servicemember by minimizing residency requirements and maximizing the ability to transfer credits between schools; and from the Defense Activity for Non-Traditional Educational Support (DANTES), a distance learning program established to serve military personnel and their particular needs. These programs are for the servicemember who wants to gain college credit and an associate or bachelor's degree. They are called nontraditional because they provide ambitious servicemembers with unique opportunities to acquire a college education.

The purpose of this guide is to make the quest for a college education easier by informing servicemembers of, and guiding them in, the many nontraditional opportunities there are to pursue a college education while on active duty.

Before starting, however, review the list of abbreviations in appendix A and study the educational definitions in appendix B. This will help you ease your way through this book.

PART I

BEGINNING THE PROCESS

1

Planning for a Civilian Education

"How do I begin?" you may ask. Your journey has already begun. Your interest in earning college credit indicates that you have the desire to improve yourself and your position in life. Reading this book demonstrates that you have the willingness to act and take the necessary positive steps toward that better life. So, you ask, what are these steps? The educational journey has been broken down into five steps:

Step 1: Establish your educational goals.

Step 2: Develop an educational plan of attack.

Step 3: Begin your educational attack.

Step 4: Monitor your success *and remain persistent.*

Step 5: Accomplish your goals, set them higher, and start again.

Using these steps will not help you work harder, but it will help you work smarter. By following them, you can accomplish any level of college education you desire.

ESTABLISH YOUR EDUCATIONAL GOALS

Establishing a goal should always be the first step in any endeavor. Before you begin a task, you must first know the objective, desired result, or goal of the task. When you took the Armed Services Vocational Aptitude Battery (ASVAB) before joining the military, you established a goal for yourself. Your goal on the ASVAB may have been simply to score high enough to meet the requirements for a specific military occupation, or your goal may have been to achieve a category I score of 93 or above. Either way, you established a goal. The same should be true with your education.

It is always easier to monitor your progress once you have a direction in life and know where you are going. So, what is your educational goal? For many servicemembers, determining their goals may be the toughest part. Many servicemembers can develop their educational goals by closely examining their career goals. Ask yourself where you want to be in your career five, ten, or fifteen years from now. By developing a clear career goal, you can easily determine a complementary educational goal. In this way, servicemembers focus on a practical application of their time and efforts that results in tangible benefits. Following are four real-life examples of complementary career and educational goals.

Example One: Petty Officer Second Class Cecilia Vega has just been promoted. She is happy about the promotion and enjoys her job, but her real desire is to become a high school algebra teacher. She joined the Navy to travel and to get money for college while serving her country. Her plan was to save as much money as possible during her four-year stint, then get out of the Navy and use the Montgomery GI Bill and her savings to attend college full-time. Petty Officer Vega's savings are not as much as she would like them to be, and she has just read about budget cutbacks in public education in her home state. To her surprise, the education officer in her unit just told her about the Troops-to-Teachers Program and how she can get a teaching job lined up before she leaves active duty. Based on this advice, Petty Officer Vega decides that she should earn her bachelor's degree before she separates from the Navy if she is to have a serious chance of pursuing her dream of being a teacher.

Her career goal: Become a high school algebra teacher.

Her educational goal: Earn her bachelor's degree.

Example Two: Gunnery Sergeant Erwin Thomas thinks that he deserves to be promoted to master sergeant. He has been in the Marine Corps for fifteen years, and during that time he has served as a drill instructor and a platoon sergeant, was deployed to Afghanistan, participated in a noncombatant evacuation operation, has consistently excelled on his fitness tests, and has always received excellent ratings from his supervisors. Promotion to master sergeant is highly competitive, and Sergeant Thomas knows that his only weakness is in his civilian education. Additionally, Sergeant Thomas has been speaking with transition counselors about his prospects for civilian employment after retirement. The counselors have strongly advised him to obtain as much college as possible before retirement. Sergeant Thomas decides that an Associate of Arts (AA) degree will both prepare him for life after the military and substantially increase his chances for promotion to master sergeant. He decides to seek and complete his AA degree during his last five years of military service.

His career goals: Earn promotion to master sergeant and prepare for retirement.

His education goal: Earn his AA degree.

Example Three: Air Force Staff Sergeant James Barber is considering applying to the Air Force Officer Training School (OTS). He has already taken some college classes and now has 96 semester hours of college. He knows that in order to apply to OTS, he must have, among other things, a bachelor's degree from a regionally accredited college. He needs another 24 semester hours before completing the final requirements for his bachelor's degree. After speaking with his squadron commander, Staff Sergeant Barber decides to pursue the quickest route to completing a bachelor's degree.

His career goal: Attend OTS and become an officer.

His educational goal: Earn his bachelor's degree.

Example Four: Army Specialist Joan Davis wants to be promoted to sergeant. Although she has not yet appeared before the promotion board, she is thinking ahead. She has already completed 18 semester hours of college. She determines that if she can max the civilian education section of her promotion point worksheet, she will be 100 points ahead of most of her peers who have not yet considered college. She also decides that the 100 points would serve as a clear indication of her desire for self-improvement when she does appear before the promotion board. Specialist Davis knows that each semester hour of college equals 1.5 promotion points in the civilian education section of the promotion point worksheet, so her 18 semester hours are worth 27 points. She needs 73 more points to max her civilian education, so she must complete another 49 semester hours of college.

Her short-term career goal: Earn promotion to sergeant.

Her education goal: Complete a total of 67 semester hours of college.

Help in Determining Your Educational Goal

If you are undecided about your career or educational goals, perhaps you need professional one-on-one guidance. Your post or base education officer can help you make your career decision with valuable career advice and counseling. Your education officer can also administer a variety of tests that measure your interest and aptitude in different fields. These tests can help point you in a direction to determine your goal. Two of these interest and aptitude tests are described below.

Career Assessment Inventory

The Career Assessment Inventory (CAI) is an objective vocational interest test that compares occupational interests and personality preferences with those of individuals in over one hundred specific careers. There is also an enhanced version of the CAI that focuses on careers requiring a secondary education. Education officers and guidance counselors use the CAI to assist those who need career guidance and adult career development. The CAI helps servicemembers focus on the interests that are important to them in making educational and occupational choices. It also assists in identifying a career direction and selecting major areas of study, advising individuals who are reentering the work force or considering a career change, screening job applicants, and providing career development assistance.

Career Planning Program

The Career Planning Program (CPP) is a guidance-oriented test designed to help individuals identify and explore relevant occupations and educational programs. This test consists of an ability test battery, an interest inventory, scales for assessing career-related experiences, and a background and plans inventory. The CPP normally takes about two and a half hours to complete and is well worth the time. The test helps counselors measure a person's interests, experience, and abilities. The CPP also uses a group guidance technique that allows the counselor to assist more people with career and educational planning. This technique is beneficial because it teaches individuals how to gather and consider information that is vital to their own career and educational planning processes. The counselors help individuals help themselves.

Keep a Diary or Journal

When considering what your goals should be, it is a good idea to keep a small notebook or diary of your ideas. Carry the notebook with you everywhere, and immediately write down any ideas that come to mind. It is also a good idea to place the notebook and a pen beside your bed at night. Think about your goals before going to sleep. Many people find that they are full of fresh ideas or struck by an inspiration upon awakening. Immediately write down any new ideas, before they are forgotten. After you have decided on your career and educational goals, write them in the notebook. You may also want to follow the advice of Olympic Decathlon Gold Medalist Dan O'Brien. He recommends that you write down your goals and carry them in your pocket. With your goals always in your mind, notebook, or pocket, you will never lose sight of the purpose of your work. Now it is time to move on to step two.

DEVELOP AN EDUCATIONAL PLAN OF ATTACK

You have developed your goals and have written them down in your notebook. You know where you are now and where you want to be. You have determined how a college education can help get you there. Now you have to tackle the next step and develop your educational plan of attack. It is important not to underestimate the need for a plan. Most military education centers now strictly enforce the requirement of a degree plan from servicemembers who desire tuition assistance.

To make it easier, step two is broken down into four smaller steps:

Step 1: Keep your plan a secret.
Step 2: Research and assess your available educational opportunities.
Step 3: Do the math and determine exactly how many credits you need.
Step 4: Make a schedule and put it in writing.

Keep Your Plan a Secret

Maintaining a positive attitude is extremely important to accomplishing any goal. It is true that most people are their own worst critic, and one critic is usually enough. Unless naysayers inspire you to work harder or you have an exceptionally high level of confidence and self-discipline, it is best to keep your plan a secret. Many people, even friends, will unintentionally drain your confidence with their doubts and negative comments. The higher or more ambitious your goals are, the more you are at risk. It makes people feel better to think that if they cannot do something, no one can. The truth is that many people feel threatened by those who try to improve themselves. Because your positive attitude is so important to success, share your intimate ideas and plans with only those whom you trust to be positive and supportive.

Research and Assess Your Available Educational Opportunities

When seeking information about your college credit opportunities, there is no substitute for firsthand knowledge, but there are shortcuts. The chapters of this book detailing nontraditional educational resources are among those shortcuts. These chapters contain firsthand knowledge gained from years of experience and research. Other sources of valuable information are the professionals at your local education center. These professionals can offer information, counseling, and advice on many of the resources covered in this book. Take advantage of their services, but read the chapters in Part V, Non-traditional Educational Resources first. These chapters will save you time, help you ask more intelligent questions, and help you zero in on those opportunities best suited to your particular situation and goals.

Do the Math and Determine Exactly What You Need

Dissect your goal and determine exactly how many credits in which courses you need to accomplish it. Do you need to earn 50 more semester hours of college to max the civilian education section of the promotion point worksheet? Do you need 100 semester hours in specific courses to complete a bachelor's degree? Using this book, the resources at your military education center, and the advice from your education officer, you can determine the component parts of your educational goal and exactly what you need to accomplish that goal. Break your goal down to the point where you know exactly which college classes and how much credit you need to earn the degree you want or the number of semester hours necessary for promotion.

Make a Schedule and Put It in Writing

You know exactly what your educational goal is, you know what opportunities exist to pursue that goal, and you have dissected and measured exactly what credits you need to accomplish your goal. Now it is time to develop a schedule for pursuing that goal (see sample schedule). A successful schedule is a catalyst to accomplishing any goal, but even more so with an educational goal. The most important parts of your schedule are the desired completion dates of your goal components. Write down a specific date by which you intend to accomplish each component of your goal. For example, write down the date you intend to take an examination for college credit or the date you intend to complete a college course over the Internet. Make the dates as practical as possible; they can be fine-tuned later as necessary. Post these dates, the components of your goal, and the goal itself in a private but noticeable place in your home or room. The refrigerator, the inside of a wall locker, your notebook, or any personal area you see daily is a good place to post these items.

BEGIN YOUR EDUCATIONAL ATTACK

By now you should have everything you need to begin your attack. You have developed a goal, you know your available resources, you have created a plan to pursue your goal, and you have made a schedule to accomplish each component of your goal by a specific date. The only thing left to do is to get started.

EDUCATION GOAL SCHEDULE
FOR SPECIALIST JOAN DAVIS
December 2002–November 2003 (1 year)

1-year career goal: promotion to sergeant
5-year career goal: undecided (but considering staying in the military)
1-year education goal: complete a total of 67 semester hours of college by November 2003
5-year education goal: undecided (considering a bachelor's degree)

	Progress toward goal of 67 semester hours
Milestones already accomplished	
Jan–Nov 2002: Completed 6 classes worth 18 semester hours	18
Sep 2002: Signed SOCAD-2 agreement with Texas Tech University	
Projected milestones	
Dec: Request AARTS transcript be sent to Texas Tech	
Jan: Receive credit for military experience (MOS and PLDC)	12
Jan: Take the General Science CLEP exam	6
Enroll in DANTES Distance Learning course	
Feb: Rotate to Bosnia for 90-day TDY (study for upcoming exams)	
Jun: Take General English CLEP (with essay) exam	6
Take Introduction to Business course at Texas Tech (8-week term)	3
Start DANTES Distance Learning course ordered in January	
Jun: Take American History I CLEP subject exam at education center	3
Jul: Take Human Resource Management ECE at education center	3
Aug: Take Business Mathematics DANTES DSST	3
Sep: Complete both distance learning courses	3
Oct: Take Sociology GRE	3–30
Nov: Take Spanish: Level 1 & 2 CLEP subject exam	6
	Total progress toward goal 66–93 semester hours

Be Prepared
Being prepared is more than a motto for the Boy Scouts; it is also one of the many secrets of success. If you have made it to this point, you already know what it means to be prepared. Part of being prepared is having a clear vision

or goal; studying and researching the problem, the obstacles, and the goal; establishing a clear path or plan to success; and implementing a schedule. In short, you are already prepared.

Be Optimistic
General Colin Powell once remarked that "perpetual optimism is a force multiplier." The spirit of optimism has been the most important factor in countless battles throughout human history, and your battle is no different. If you lose your can-do attitude, you will lose the battle.

Be Disciplined
Remember, no one can do it for you. You have to be committed to sticking to your schedule. If your schedule dictates that you study two hours each day in preparation for an online college course, you must study two hours. Put your schedule ahead of all other unnecessary activities. If you are serious, then your studying will take first priority over entertainment, television, and beer with your buddies. Everyone has heard that if you want something badly enough, you should be willing to work for it. If this is not true of your educational goals, then you probably do not want them badly enough. At the same time, do not overdo it. If you tend to be a workaholic, remember to take breaks and enjoy life. The idea is to be disciplined enough to work as hard as necessary to accomplish your goal without inducing burnout.

MONITOR YOUR SUCCESS AND REMAIN PERSISTENT
It is important to monitor the success, or lack thereof, of all your efforts. Again, optimism is extremely important, but it may be unrealistic to expect to accomplish everything you strive for on the first try. You must be prepared to modify your plan and your schedule based on your positive and negative experiences. If you are ahead of schedule, then perhaps you have room for a more ambitious goal. If you are behind schedule, then perhaps you were overly optimistic. Review your efforts at least once a week, and make notes about both your successes and your failures in the personal goals' notebook mentioned earlier. Continually monitoring your efforts is important to success, as it allows you to maximize lessons learned from both success and failure.

Failure, as well as success, is part of the process of pursuing your goal. The objective is to remain persistent and optimistic and to realize that more is often gained from failure than from success. When you broke your educational goal down into component parts, you were reducing your goal to the lowest denominator. The lowest denominator is important because it represents the small steps toward your goal. Remain persistent and do something every day, even if it takes only five minutes, to push onward toward your educational goal. By remaining persistent, you will notice that your small steps add up quickly, and before you know it, you will have traveled miles toward your goal.

ACCOMPLISH YOUR GOALS, SET THEM HIGHER, AND START AGAIN

By following the steps outlined in the previous pages, using the information in this book, and following the advice of the professional counselors at your military education center, you can accomplish your educational goals. Then, once you have done this, the only step left will be to set your goals even higher and start again.

2

Educational Opportunities and Resources

The opportunities available to servicemembers who want to pursue a college education while on active duty are almost limitless. However, many servicemembers believe that on-campus daytime courses taught at a local college are the only option. Although this is the most common, traditional way to obtain college credit, it is only one of many. In fact, there are hundreds of nontraditional sources and opportunities available for servicemembers who want to earn college credit.

THE DIFFERENCE BETWEEN TRADITIONAL AND NONTRADITIONAL EDUCATIONAL PROGRAMS

Traditional educational programs consist of on-campus daytime courses taught at a local college or university. There are nearly 10,000 such postsecondary schools in the United States. These colleges and universities cater mostly to a young student body. Their programs are rigid, with institutionally structured rules and regulations designed for less mature men and women. Usually these students attend school full-time, and often they have no other responsibilities. Many of these colleges and universities offer classes that are available only during the daytime to full-time students.

The nontraditional college education breaks with the concept that all learning must occur at a young age in a daytime classroom setting. The nontraditional opportunities include, but are not limited to, evening classes, online courses, weekend classes, summer classes, independent study, correspondence courses, video classes, telecourses, contract learning, college credit by examination, and college credit for life experience.

You will have to decide which route is best for you. If you are a servicemember on active duty, however, your opportunities to pursue college traditionally are limited by the nature of your military duties. When most servicemembers complain they cannot pursue college credit, they are refer-ring to college credit obtained by traditional methods. Most servicemembers are not aware that there are nontraditional ways to pursue the same college education they could by using the traditional route. Nontraditional methods are also easier, cheaper, less utilized, and less publicized.

This book, therefore, was specifically written to promote the educa-tional opportunities available through *nontraditional* educational methods, with emphasis on describing all educational resources available to the ser-vicemember. Each service has a slightly different name for its nontraditional educational programs, but each service program uses three ways to help you get college credits toward promotion or a formal degree:

1. College credit for military experience. The U.S. Armed Forces is one of the most highly trained sectors of American society. Much of the military training you have already received may be eligible for col-lege credits, which then equates to formal academic course work that you may not need to take. More at chapter 10.
2. College credit by taking examinations. There are many examination programs for college-level subjects. Often, by taking an examination of your knowledge of the subject matter, you could be awarded col-lege credit for the course. More at chapter 11.
3. College credits from course work, either in the traditional classroom setting or via nontraditional methods, such as over the Internet or from correspondence courses. You will have to take some formal course work to meet your educational goals or to meet the academic requirements of the degree you are seeking, but the military programs for doing this are extensive, convenient, and geared to the military profession and duty environment. Most of this book discusses these programs.

NONTRADITIONAL EDUCATIONAL RESOURCES

Listed below are some of the largest, easiest to use, and cheapest resources of nontraditional college credit available to servicemembers, including reserve and National Guard personnel, who may use any of the programs that are applicable to their military service. Each resource is covered in detail in subsequent chapters.

College Credits from Military Experience

Army/American Council on Education Registry Transcript System: college credit for Army experience.

Army University Access Online (eArmyU): colleges with unique degree programs for soldiers and online laptop-based courses.

Sailor/Marine American Council on Education Registry Transcript: college credit for Navy and Marine Corps experience.

Navy College Program for Afloat College Education: academic skills and college courses for sailors and marines while on sea duty.

Community College of the Air Force: college for enlisted personnel that awards college credit for Air Force experience.

DD Form 295, *Application for Evaluation of Learning Experiences during Military Service*: college credit for military experience.

DD Form 2586, *Verification of Military Experience and Training*: college credit for military experience.

College Credits from Examinations (Tests) of Knowledge You Already Have

Annenberg Program: video preparation for college credit examinations.

College Level Examination Program (CLEP) tests: college credit by examination.

Defense Activity for Non-Traditional Educational Support (DANTES) examinations: college credit by examination.

Excelsior College Examinations: college credit by examination.

Graduate Record Examination (GRE) tests: undergraduate curricula achievement/graduate school entrance examinations used by some institutions to award college credit.

Credits from Nontraditional Course Work

DANTES Distance Learning Program: college credit for courses offered through the mail, on video, or online.

Excelsior College: nontraditional college with unique degree completion programs.

Military education center and other resources: miscellaneous programs and information on many other nontraditional programs.

Servicemember Opportunity Colleges: colleges with unique degree completion programs and contract learning designed for military personnel.

Thomas Edison State College: nontraditional college with unique degree completion programs.

PART II

ARMY PROGRAMS

3

College Credit for
Army Experience: AARTS

The Army/American Council on Education (ACE) Registry Transcript System (AARTS) compiles a transcript that is an official record of your military education and is used to translate your military experience into college credit. It lists most of your active-duty military training courses and educational experiences in a format similar to that of transcripts from a high school or college. In addition, the AARTS transcript includes the ACE college credit recommendations for each of the military courses and experiences listed.

The purpose of the AARTS transcript is to facilitate the awarding of college credit to soldiers for their completed military courses and training. Most colleges and universities award college credit for military training in accordance with the recommendations found in the *Guide to the Evaluation of Educational Experiences in the Armed Services,* published by ACE. The Army and ACE cooperate to maintain the AARTS. A transcript from AARTS saves college officials time, ensures the accuracy of ACE recommendations, and allows colleges to award credit more easily to soldiers for their training and experience.

INFORMATION INCLUDED ON THE AARTS TRANSCRIPT
The AARTS transcript includes important information about a soldier's military career and experiences. The transcript is divided into the following sections:

Biographical data: the soldier's name, social security number, rank, military status, time in service, and highest academic level completed.

Test scores: CLEP, American College Testing Proficiency Examination Program (ACT-PEP), Excelsior College Examination (ECE), SAT, and DANTES Subject Standardized Test (DSST) scores; test dates; test numbers; test titles; and the Army/American Council on Education recommended college credit for each test taken through DANTES or a military education center.

Military course descriptions: entries for basic training and advanced individual training (AIT) courses completed; completed Noncommissioned Officer Education System (NCOES) courses, such as the Primary Leadership Development Course (PLDC), Basic NCO Course (BNCOC), and Advanced NCO Course (ANCOC); other completed formal service school courses that were longer than 45 hours; course titles; course locations; dates of attendance; course descriptions; Army and ACE course identification numbers; and the ACE recommended college credit for each course.

Military experience: all primary, secondary, and duty military occupational specialties (MOSs) held by the soldier; duty descriptions for all MOSs performed; and the ACE recommended college credit.

Other learning experiences: data on any completed courses that are pending evaluation by the Army/American Council on Education, completed courses with information not yet available in the computer system, or completed courses that ACE is not able to evaluate.

INFORMATION NOT INCLUDED ON THE AARTS TRANSCRIPT

Currently, the AARTS transcript does not include information on correspondence courses; local command training courses; headstart courses; training or experience information for reserve components; or training, courses, or experience in other branches of the military, other government agencies, or civilian organizations.

Military courses not included on the AARTS transcript may be documented using DD Form 295, which is covered in chapter 10. A transcript of military courses taught or offered through the Air Force may be requested from the Community College of the Air Force, which is covered in chapter 8. Most government and civilian agencies will also provide a transcript of any courses completed with their organizations. Before writing to request a transcript, however, it is good to call and verify the cost and proper mailing address. Even some government agencies charge transcript fees.

ARMY/AMERICAN COUNCIL ON EDUCATION
REGISTRY TRANSCRIPT

06/15/02   ** PERSONAL COPY **   PAGE 1

TRANSCRIPT SENT TO: NAME: DOE JOHN DAVID
                                              SSN: 123-45-6789
                                              RANK: SPECIALIST
SPC JOHN DOE   MILITARY STATUS: ACTIVE
9876 MAIN STREET   TIME IN SERVICE:
WASHINGTON DC 20340   3 YEARS, 5 MONTHS
                                              ACADEMIC LEVEL COMPLETED:
                                                  2 YR COLLEGE
AARTS ID: 02-12345
----------------------- MILITARY COURSE COMPLETIONS ----------------------

COURSE: BASIC TRAINING   ACE GUIDE ID NUMBER:
            (RECRUIT TRAINING)   AR-2201-0399

DESCRIPTION: UPON COMPLETION OF THIS PROGRAM OF INSTRUCTION, THE GRADUATED
RECRUIT WILL BE ABLE TO DEMONSTRATE: 1) GENERAL KNOWLEDGE OF MILITARY
ORGANIZATION AND CULTURE; 2) MASTERY OF INDIVIDUAL AND GROUP COMBAT SKILLS
INCLUDING MARKSMANSHIP AND FIRST AID; 3) ACHIEVEMENT OF MINIMAL PHYSICAL
CONDITIONING STANDARDS; AND 4) ABILITY TO SUCCESSFULLY APPLY BASIC SAFETY
AND LIVING SKILLS IN THE OUTDOOR ENVIRONMENT. INSTRUCTION INCLUDES
LECTURES, DEMONSTRATIONS, AND PERFORMANCE EXERCISES IN BASIC MILITARY
CULTURE/SUBJECTS INCLUDING MARKSMANSHIP, PHYSICAL CONDITIONING, FIRST AID
AND OUTDOOR ADAPTATION/LIVING SKILLS.

ACE CREDIT RECOMMENDATION: IN THE LOWER-DIVISION BACCALAUREATE/ASSOCIATE
DEGREE CATEGORY, 1 SEMESTER HOUR IN PERSONAL PHYSICAL CONDITIONING, 1 IN
OUTDOOR SKILLS PRACTICUM, 1 IN MARKSMANSHIP, AND 1 IN FIRST AID.

COURSE: PRIMARY LEADERSHIP DEVELOPMENT   ACE GUIDE ID NUMBER:
            NCO ACADEMY   AR-2201-0253
            FT STEWART, GA

DATES TAKEN: 11/21/01-12/20/01 ARMY COURSE NUMBER: 698-04-PLDC

DESCRIPTION: UPON COMPLETION OF THE COURSE, THE STUDENT WILL BE ABLE TO
PERFORM ALL BASIC TASKS RELATING TO THE NONCOMMISSIONED OFFICER LEADERSHIP
RESPONSIBILITY. LECTURES AND PRACTICAL EXERCISES IN LEADERSHIP,
COMMUNICATIONS, RESOURCE MANAGEMENT, TRAINING MANAGEMENT, AND PROFESSIONAL
SKILLS, INCLUDING INTRODUCTION TO LEADERSHIP, PRINCIPLES OF LEADERSHIP,
HUMAN BEHAVIOR, CHARACTER OF LEADERS, ETHICS, PROBLEM SOLVING, LEADERSHIP
STYLES, PRINCIPLES OF MOTIVATION, COUNSELING, AND RESPONSIBILITY OF
AUTHORITY. EMPHASIS IS ON TEACHING TO TEACH AND TO LEAD SOLDIERS WHO WILL
WORK AND FIGHT UNDER THEIR LEADERSHIP. COURSE CONTENT INCLUDES DEFENSIVE/
**************************** CONTINUED ON PAGE 2 ****************************

ARMY/AMERICAN COUNCIL ON EDUCATION REGISTRY TRANSCRIPT

06/15/02   ** PERSONAL COPY **   PAGE 2

TRANSCRIPT SENT TO: NAME: DOE JOHN DAVID
SPC JOHN DOE   SSN: 123-45-6789
9876 MAIN STREET
WASHINGTON DC 20340

----------------------- MILITARY COURSE COMPLETIONS ---------------------
OFFENSIVE OPERATIONS, AND FIELD TRAINING EXERCISES IN WHICH PREVIOUS
LESSONS ARE APPLIED.

ACE CREDIT RECOMMENDATION: IN THE LOWER-DIVISION BACCALAUREATE/ASSOCIATE
DEGREE CATEGORY, 1 SEMESTER HOUR IN PRINCIPLES OF SUPERVISION, 2 IN
MILITARY SCIENCE.

------------------------------ TEST SCORES ------------------------------

DANTES SUBJECT STANDARDIZED TESTS (DSST)

     -    SE470   GEOGRAPHY
DATE: 05/18/99   SCORE: 064 ACE RECOMMENDED PASSING SCORE: 046
                                 ACE RECOMMENDED CREDIT: 03 SH

COLLEGE LEVEL EXAMINATION PROGRAM (CLEP) - GENERAL

     -    03191   MATHEMATICS
DATE: 05/11/99   SCORE: 626 MS: 63   MC: 63
ACE RECOMMENDED PASSING SCORE: 421   ACE RECOMMENDED CREDIT: 06 SH

--------------------------- MILITARY EXPERIENCE -------------------------

MILITARY OCCUPATIONAL SPECIALTIES HELD: 98C10 PRIMARY   (07/99-06/02)
                                         98C10 DUTY

MILITARY OCCUPATIONAL SPECIALTY GROUP: 98C   ACE GUIDE ID NUMBER:
TITLE: SIGNALS INTELLIGENCE ANALYST   MOS 98C-003
        (SIGINT ANALYST)
DESCRIPTION OF 98C10: GATHERS, SORTS, AND SCANS INTERCEPTED MESSAGES AND
SIGNALS, AND PERFORMS INITIAL ANALYSIS TO ESTABLISH COMMUNICATIONS
PATTERNS; ISOLATES VALID MESSAGE TRAFFIC; REDUCES COMMUNICATIONS DATA INTO
AUTOMATIC DATA PROCESSING FORMAT; OPERATES COMMUNICATIONS EQUIPMENT FOR
************************** CONTINUED ON PAGE 3 **************************

ARMY/AMERICAN COUNCIL ON EDUCATION
REGISTRY TRANSCRIPT

06/15/02   ** PERSONAL COPY **   PAGE 3

TRANSCRIPT SENT TO: NAME: DOE JOHN DAVID
SPC JOHN DOE   SSN: 123-45-6789
9876 MAIN STREET
WASHINGTON DC 20340

--------------------------- MILITARY EXPERIENCE ---------------------------

REPORTING AND COORDINATION; TYPES AT A MINIMUM RATE OF 24 WORDS PER MINUTE;
HAS KNOWLEDGE OF THE GEOGRAPHY AND CULTURE OF THE AREA FROM WHICH
INTERCEPTED COMMUNICATIONS ORIGINATE; MAY ACQUIRE A TECHNICAL VOCABULARY IN
ONE OR MORE FOREIGN LANGUAGE(S).

ACE CREDIT RECOMMENDATION FOR 98C10: IN THE VOCATIONAL CERTIFICATE
CATEGORY, 3 SEMESTER HOURS IN ELECTRONIC SYSTEMS OPERATIONS. IN THE LOWER-
DIVISION BACCALAUREATE/ASSOCIATE DEGREE CATEGORY, 3 SEMESTER HOURS IN
WRITTEN COMMUNICATIONS, 3 IN KEYBOARDING, 1 IN COMPUTER LITERACY, AND 2 IN
GEOGRAPHY, AND CREDIT FOR FOREIGN LANGUAGE PROFICIENCY ON THE BASIS OF
INSTITUTIONAL EVALUATION.

----------------------- OTHER LEARNING EXPERIENCES -----------------------

COURSE NUMBER/   COURSE TITLE/
DATES TAKEN   COURSE LOCATION

--------------------   --------------------

X3AB420230-001 (98C10)   EW/CRYPTOLOGIC TRAFFIC ANALYST
03/20/99-/07/14/99   USAF TECHNICAL TRAINING SCHOOL
                                   GOODFELLOW AFB, TX

************ LAST ENTRY ********** PAGE 3 OF 3 ********************

OBTAINING A COPY OF YOUR AARTS TRANSCRIPT

The AARTS transcript is free. To obtain a copy of your transcript, pick up DA Form 5454-R, *Request for Army/American Council on Education Registry Transcript*, from your education center and mail it to AARTS Operations Center, Fort Leavenworth, KS 66027-5073. You can also send the request via fax: (913) 684-2011. If you can not obtain DA Form 5454-R, write a letter requesting your AARTS transcript and send it to the address or fax number above. Be sure that all requests include your full name, social security number, basic active service date, and the address or addresses where you would like AARTS to send your transcript. If you do not already have a copy of your AARTS transcript, you should request one immediately.

No ambitious noncommissioned officer ever allows his or her records to appear before a promotion or selection board without first reviewing them to ensure that they are 100 percent accurate and up-to-date. The same should be true for your educational records. The people at AARTS do an excellent job, but mistakes are made occasionally. Additionally, it may take AARTS up to three months to update your records after promotion, course completions, and other changes. Regardless of the reason, the earlier a mistake is discovered, the easier it is to correct.

MAKING CORRECTIONS TO YOUR AARTS TRANSCRIPT

If you discover errors in your AARTS transcript, write a letter detailing the errors and mail it to AARTS Operations Center, Fort Leavenworth, KS 66027-5073. As with the request for your transcript, this letter should include your full name, social security number, basic active service date, and the address or addresses where you would like AARTS to send the corrected transcript. Be sure to include with your letter certified copies of documents that refute the errors. A certified copy of your DA Form 2A, *Personnel Qualification Record Part I*; DA Form 2-1, *Personnel Qualification Record Part II*; DA Form 1059, *Service School Academic Evaluation Report*, or your course completion certificates will generally suffice to correct most errors.

AARTS TRANSCRIPT USE

The AARTS transcript can be a valuable supplement or attachment to the resume of a retiring or separating soldier, but the transcript itself is not a resume. Because the AARTS transcript includes military experiences and job descriptions, it can be an important tool for those seeking to provide potential employers with a complete understanding of their military skills and responsibilities.

Only enlisted Army personnel and veterans can use AARTS to request a transcript. Members of the Army Reserve, warrant officers, commissioned officers, and members of other services cannot receive AARTS transcripts. Additionally, soldiers are not eligible to receive an AARTS transcript if they have a basic active service date (BASD) of 30 September 1981 or earlier. If you are not eligible to use AARTS, you can still use DD Form 295 to request evaluation of your military training and experience.

4

Army University Access Online Program: eArmyU

The Army University Access Online (AUAO) Program, known as *eArmyU*, enables enlisted soldiers to obtain professional technical certifications and associate, bachelor's, and master's degrees using laptop computers to access online courses while they serve in the Army. eArmyU offers a broad range of high-quality programs to help train soldiers in their current career or prepare them for a new one. It is designed to offer the enlisted soldiers the opportunity to complete a college degree or certificate anytime, anywhere. eArmyU offers soldiers access to accredited colleges, universities, and technical schools at no cost. Soldiers can choose from more than ninety degree programs to fulfill their educational and career goals.

HOW eArmyU WORKS
Soldiers participating in the Army University Access Online Program are provided with all the tools they need to operate as an online student in a technology package training session, which they are scheduled to attend when they enroll in the program and register for a course. As part of the technology package, soldiers are issued a laptop computer for accessing their courses, a printer, Internet service provider and e-mail accounts, and live technology support that includes on-site specialists, a call center help desk, and computer training. After a soldier completes a minimum number of online courses, the laptop and printer become the property of the soldier.

With eArmyU, soldiers can earn their certificate or degree from a home institution while taking courses from multiple colleges and universities. The home institution evaluates the students' prior learning experiences, including military training and experience and college-level testing, for maximum credit toward their program of study. Credits transfer across institutions, allowing soldiers to earn their degree as quickly and conveniently as possible.

The AUAO Program is built around the eArmyU web portal, where participating soldiers can access course work, educational advisory services, online registration services, and online technical and administrative support. It is also the doorway through which Army education counselors, program mentors, and others access tools that enable them to provide online support to students. The portal also provides Army officials, universities, and eArmyU staff with access to program data.

IS eArmyU A SELF-STUDY PROGRAM?

eArmyU is not a self-study program. Soldiers enrolled in it have comprehensive support from a variety of sources before and during their enrollment in the program. Army education counselors work to ensure that soldiers enroll in the degree program appropriate to their needs and academic level. Once enrolled, soldiers receive assistance from program mentors who work closely with Army education counselors to monitor and track the students' progress and to manage issues with institutions regarding credit for military experience and training and standardized testing. Online tutoring services are also available to students, and for some courses, instructors or course tutors may review course work and conduct online review sessions. Finally, course-level support is augmented by online writing and research tools and online tutoring and academic support for core courses, such as mathematics, statistics, economics, and accounting. Participating soldiers receive one hour of free tutoring per course.

AUAO ELIGIBILITY

To be eligible to use AUAO/eArmyU, a prospective student must be a regular active-duty, active guard, or active reserve enlisted soldier with a high school diploma or GED (General Educational Development) certificate. Soldiers must be physically assigned to a participating installation, not have a pending permanent-change-of-station assignment, have three years remaining on their enlistment, and meet the school's admissions criteria. Finally, soldiers who desire to participate in eArmyU must be counseled by an Army education counselor, have the approval of the unit commander, and sign an AUAO participation agreement. Soldiers who meet the eligibility requirements can apply at the eArmyU website at *www.eArmyU.com*.

SCHOOLS PARTICIPATING IN THE eArmyU PROGRAM
The following schools participate in eArmyU:
Anne Arundel Community College
Baker College
Central Texas College
Cochise College
Embry-Riddle Aeronautical University
Excelsior College
Fayetteville Technical Community College
Franklin University
Kansas State University
Lansing Community College
North Carolina Agricultural and Technical State University
Northern Virginia Community College
Northwest Missouri State University
Nova Southeastern University
Pennsylvania State University World Campus
Rio Salado Community College
Saint Joseph's College of Maine
Saint Leo University
State University of New York Empire State College
Thomas Edison State College
Troy State University
University of Texas at Arlington
University of the Incarnate Word
Utah State University

DEGREES OFFERED BY eArmyU
The following certificate and degree programs are offered in the eArmyU
Program:

Anne Arundel Community College
Associate of Applied Science in Business Administration
Associate of Applied Science in Business Management
Associate of Arts in General Studies

Baker College
Bachelor of Business Administration in General Business
Bachelor of Business Administration in Human Resource Management
Bachelor of Health Service Administration

Certificate of Completion in Web Design
Master of Business Administration

Central Texas College
Associate of Applied Science in Applied Technology
Associate of Applied Science in Business Management
Associate of Applied Science in Criminal Justice
Associate of Applied Science in General Studies
Associate of Applied Science in Hospitality Management
Certificate of Completion in Business Management
Certificate of Completion in Criminal Justice
Certificate of Completion in Hospitality Management

Cochise College
Certificate of Completion in International Business
Certificate of Completion in Unix

Embry-Riddle Aeronautical University
Associate of Applied Science in Professional Aeronautics
Bachelor of Science in Management Technology Operations
Bachelor of Science in Professional Aeronautics

Excelsior College
Master of Arts in Liberal Studies
Master of Science in Nursing

Fayetteville Technical Community College
Associate of Applied Science in Business Administration

Franklin University
Bachelor of Science in Business Administration
Bachelor of Science in Computer Science
Bachelor of Science in Healthcare Management
Bachelor of Science in Management Information Systems
Bachelor of Science in Public Safety Management
Bachelor of Science in Technical Management
Master of Business Administration in Business Administration

Kansas State University
Bachelor of Science in General Business

Lansing Community College
Associate of Applied Science in General Business
Certificate of Completion in Internet for Business

North Carolina Agricultural and Technical State University
Bachelor of Science in Occupational Safety and Health

Northern Virginia Community College
Associate of Applied Science in General Studies

Northwest Missouri State University
Bachelor of Science in Accounting
Bachelor of Science in Management

Nova Southeastern University
Bachelor of Science in Professional Management
Master of Business Administration
Master of Science in Computer Information Systems
Master of Science in Management Information Systems

Pennsylvania State University World Campus
Master of Education in Adult Education

Rio Salado Community College
Associate of Applied Science in Computer Technology
Associate of Applied Science in General Studies
Associate of Arts in General
Certificate of Completion in Computer Helpdesk
Certificate of Completion in Computer Technology
Certificate of Completion in Desktop Publishing
Certificate of Completion in Networking
Certificate of Completion in Organizational Leadership
Certificate of Completion in Programming
Certificate of Completion in Quality Customer Service
Certificate of Completion in Technology Troubleshooting
Certificate of Completion in Web Master

Saint Joseph's College of Maine
Bachelor of Science in Healthcare Administration

Bachelor of Science in Long-Term Care Administration
Bachelor of Science in Professional Arts
Certificate of Completion in Healthcare Management
Certificate of Completion in Long-Term Care/Administration
Master of Science in Health Services Administration

Saint Leo University
Bachelor of Arts in Accounting
Bachelor of Arts in Business Administration
Bachelor of Science in Computer Information Systems

State University of New York Empire State College
Bachelor of Science in Business, Management, and Economics

Thomas Edison State College
Associate of Applied Science and Technology in Computer Science
   Technology
Associate of Applied Science in General Management
Associate of Arts
Bachelor of Arts
Bachelor of Arts in Liberal Studies
Bachelor of Science in Business Administration
Master of Arts in Professional Studies
Master of Science in Management

Troy State University
Associate of Applied Science in Business Administration
Associate of Applied Science in General Education
Bachelor of Applied Science in Resource Management
Bachelor of Science in Criminal Justice
Bachelor of Science in Management

University of the Incarnate Word
Bachelor of Arts in Psychology of Organization and Development
Bachelor of Business Administration
Certificate of Completion in International Business
Certificate of Completion in Organizational Development
Master of Arts in Administration
Master of Business Administration

University of Texas at Arlington
Master of Business Administration

Utah State University
Master of Science English

IS THE AUAO/eArmyU PROGRAM REALLY FREE?

Eligible soldiers receive 100 percent funding for tuition, books, and course fees, up to $4,500 per year, but they must pay for their telephone service. Soldiers must successfully complete 12 semester hours of AUAO courses during their first two years of AUAO participation. Failure to successfully complete the required courses requires repayment of the prorated value of the technology package. As with current tuition assistance programs, the soldier must reimburse the government for the cost of failed courses or those courses that the soldier does not complete for reasons other than military reasons, as certified by the unit commander.

Soldiers can obtain the latest information about programs and availability at the AUAO website: *www.eArmyU.com.*

PART III

NAVY–MARINE CORPS PROGRAMS

5

College Credit for Navy and Marine Corps Experience: SMART

The Sailor/Marine American Council on Education Registry Transcript (SMART) is an academically accepted record that is validated by the American Council on Education (ACE). It compiles a transcript that is an official record of your military service and is used to translate your military experience into college credit. It lists your active-duty military training courses and educational experiences.

The purpose of SMART is to assist sailors and marines in obtaining college credit for their military experiences by making recommendations for college credit based on the *Guide to the Evaluation of Learning Experiences in the Armed Services*. A transcript from SMART saves college officials time, ensures the accuracy of ACE recommendations, and allows colleges to award credit more easily to sailors and marines for their training and experience. The SMART will eventually replace DD Form 295, *Application for Evaluation of Learning Experiences during Military Service*, which is the form sailors and marines currently submit to colleges to verify their military experiences. DD Form 295 is discussed in chapter 10.

All active-duty and reserve officer and enlisted sailors and marines and those who separated or retired from active duty after 30 September 1999 may use SMART.

INFORMATION INCLUDED ON THE SMART

The SMART contains all of the important information needed to convert the military experience and training of sailors and marines into college credit. It details the ACE college credit recommendations for military occupations

held by sailors and marines, including ratings, military occupational specialties (MOSs), certain Navy enlisted classifications (NECs), and limited duty
officer/chief warrant officer (LDO/CWO) specialties. It also lists information
about military training courses completed—including courses taken with
other military services and Department of Defense organizations, as long as
that information has been recorded in the official course database maintained
by the Navy and Marine Corps; college-level examinations taken at military
testing sites; and information about military courses taken for which there
are no matching ACE credit recommendations. The transcript is divided into
the following sections:

Biographical data: the name of the sailor or marine, social security
number, and rank.

Military course completions: entries for all Navy and Marine Corps
courses completed, such as basic military training, advanced technical courses, instructor courses, and petty officer leadership courses;
course titles; ACE identifiers; locations; military course identifiers;
dates taken; course descriptions; and the ACE college credit recommendation for each course.

Military experience: all military occupations held, ACE identifiers,
occupation identifiers, job descriptions, and the ACE-recommended
college credit.

College-level test scores: CLEP, ACT-PEP, ECEs, and DSST scores for
all tests taken at a military testing site; test dates; test numbers; test
titles; and the ACE-recommended college credit for each test.

Other learning experiences: data on any completed courses that have
not been evaluated by ACE, courses where class attendance dates
were not recorded in the servicemember's record, courses not completed during the ACE evaluation period, or courses not evaluated
by ACE at specific locations.

Summary transcript: an addendum to SMART that provides a stream-
lined overview of all the credits ACE recommends in a format that
closely resembles many college transcripts. It also contains Servicemembers Opportunity Colleges (SOC) course category codes,
which help academic institution counselors determine where the
credit will apply in established degree programs at SOC institutions.

Academic institution page: another addendum that lists college courses
taken while on active duty using tuition assistance (TA) or the Navy
College Program for Afloat College Education (NCPACE) or from
the Community College of the Air Force (CCAF).

Doe, Jane T.   123-45-6789   Page 1 of 4

SAILOR/MARINE
AMERICAN COUNCIL ON EDUCATION
REGISTRY TRANSCRIPT

INDIVIDUAL COPY

Transcript Sent To:
Jane T. Doe

Name: **Doe, Jane T.**
SSN: **123-45-6789**
Rank: Aviation Support Equipment Technician, First
Class

Military Course Completions

Course: Basic Military Training (Recruit Training)

ACE Identifier:
NV-2202-0014
Military Course ID:
X-777-7770

Date Taken: 09-DEC-1985
Description:
Student receives indoctrination and physical conditioning to prepare for the rigors and unique demands of naval service. Observance of naval customs and traditions is taught in a manner to foster pride in the nation and in patriotic behavior, high standards of conduct, and respect for civilian and military authority.
ACE Credit Recommendation:
In the lower-division baccalaureate/associate degree category, 1 semester hour in personal fitness/conditioning, 1 in personal/community health, and 2 in first aid and safety (10/79).

Course: Enlisted Basic Aviation Training (Aviation Fundamentals, Class AP)
Naval Air Technical Training Center
Millington, TN

ACE Identifier:
NV-1704-0157
Military Course ID:
C-000-2010

Date Taken: 11-FEB-1986 To   24-FEB-1986
Description:
To train personnel in aviation mechanical fundamentals. Self-paced instruction with practical exercises in aviation mechanical fundamentals, including general information, use of hand tools, torquing, safetying aircraft hardware and general mathematics.
ACE Credit Recommendation:
In the lower-division baccalaureate/associate degree category, 1 semester hour in aircraft fundamentals or maintenance technician (2/81).

09/07/2002

** PRIVACY ACT INFORMATION **

Doe, Jane T.   **123-45-6789**   **Page 2 of 4**

Course: Aviation Support Equipment Technician (Mechanical), Class A   **ACE Identifier:**
Naval Air Technical Training Center   NV-1704-0246
Millington, TN   **Military Course ID:**
          C-602-2025
Date Taken: 18-MAR-1986   To   01-JUL-1986
Description:
To train enlisted personnel in the maintenance, operation, and repair of aircraft support vehicles and
equipment. Lectures and laboratory instruction in the repair, overhaul, and troubleshooting of gasoline
and diesel engines, electrical systems and related hydraulic systems. Instruction and shop practices in gas
and arc welding.

ACE Credit Recommendation:
In the lower-division baccalaureate/associate degree category, 2 semester hours in gasoline engines, 1 in
diesel engines, 2 in basic electricity, 1 in basic hydraulic systems, 1 in oxyacetylene welding, and 1 in
electric-arc welding (2/85).

Course: P-3 T56-A-10/14 Engine and Related Systems Organizational   **ACE Identifier:**
Maintenance (P-3 T-56-A-14 Engine and Related Systems Maint)   NV-1704-0028
Air Station   **Military Course ID:**
Jacksonville, FL   C-602-3238

Date Taken: 18-AUG-1986   To   12-SEP-1986
Description:
Lectures and practical exercises cover the maintenance and repair of internal combustion engine charging,
starting, and ignition systems, including battery analysis and basic theory, analysis, troubleshooting, and
repair of generators, regulators, alternators, starters, and ignition systems using special test equipment
such as a dwell meter, growler, and oscilloscope.

ACE Credit Recommendation:
In the lower-division baccalaureate/associate degree category, 1 semester hour in automotive or aircraft
electrical systems and 1 in automotive or aircraft electrical laboratory for non-electrical engineering
students (3/82).

Course: First Class Petty Officer Leadership   **ACE Identifier:**
Aviation Schools Command   NV-1717-0027
Pensacola FL   **Military Course ID:**
          P-500-0020
Date Taken: 10-AUG-1998   To   21-AUG-1998
Description:
Upon completion of the course, the student will be able to identify basic principles of leadership
including the use oral and written communication in professional relationships; the role of motivation,
empowerment, and counseling in subordinate development; ways to manage human resources, teams, and
stress to create a quality organizational climate.

09/07/2002

** PRIVACY ACT INFORMATION **

Doe, Jane T.   123-45-6789   **Page 3 of 4**

ACE Credit Recommendation:
In the lower-division baccalaureate/associate degree category, 2 semester hours in personnel supervision or 1 in leadership and 1 in business and professional communication. Credit duplicates that in P-500-0021, and P-500-0025 (8/97).

Military Experience

Occupation: Airman Recruit

ACE Identifier:
*NONE ASSIGNED
Occupation ID:
NER-AR

Description:
To assimilate recruits into the Navy way of life and to prepare them for further advanced training in specialized Navy occupations.

ACE Credit Recommendation:
None

Occupation: Aviation Support Equipment Technician

ACE Identifier:
NER-AS-003
Occupation ID:
AS1

Description:
Performs preventive and corrective maintenance on aviation ground support equipment, mobile fire fighting units, material handling and moving units; inspects and repairs gasoline, diesel and turbine ground power units; services transmissions, hydraulic and pneumatic systems, cryogenic and air conditioning equipment; performs troubleshooting and repair of electrical control and motors; replaces electrical generating components; adjusts mechanical and electrical regulators; provides training and work schedules; manages distribution and maintenance schedules for ground support equipment at different command levels. Analyzes and diagnoses malfunctions of the hydraulics, pneumatic, electrical power generating, chassis and chassis electrical systems and internal combustion engines and air conditioning and gas turbine compressors; determines corrective action; maintains shop files and technical publications; plans shop work schedule; supervises subordinates; performs quality control inspections; prepares schedules of preventive maintenance; requisitions and is responsible for materials and equipment.

ACE Credit Recommendation:
In the lower-division baccalaureate/associate degree category, 3 semester hours in basic shop practices, 3 in basic electricity, 2 in diesel engines, 2 in basic hydraulics, 2 in electric generators, 2 in electric control systems, 1 in shop management, 2 in records and information management, 2 in personnel supervision, and 2 in maintenance management.

*NONE ASSIGNED--Occupation not evaluated by ACE or not evaluated during time frame held by servicemember.

09/07/2002
** PRIVACY ACT INFORMATION **

College Level Test Scores

College Level Examination Program (CLEP)

Date Taken	Title	Recmd Hrs	Required by ACE	Student's Score	Sub Score1	Sub Score2	Verbal Score
15-JUL-1992	Spanish: Level 1 & 2	6 or 12	41	74	71	75	

Other Learning Experiences

This section provides a record of the service member's learning experiences that do not have credit recommended for one or more of the following reasons:
(1) The course has not been evaluated by ACE
(2) The class attendance date were not recorded in the service member's record
(3) The course was not completed during the ACE evaluation period
(4) The course was not evaluated by ACE at this specific location

J-495-0412	08-SEP-1988	General Shipboard Fire Fighting	Fleet Training Center Norfolk VA	1
J-495-0412	28-OCT-1993	General Shipboard Fire Fighting	Fleet Training Center San Diego CA	1
P-500-0034	02-FEB-1996	Navy Leader Development Program Leading Petty Officer	Naval Leadership Training Unit Coronado San Diego CA	1
C-602-3263	12-JUL-1996	Aviation Support Equipment Technician Electrical	Naval Air Maintenance Training Group Det, NAS North Island San Diego CA	1
C-602-3307	16-AUG-1996	A/S-32A/35 and A/S-32A/36 Crash Cranes Intermediate Maintenance	Naval Air Maintenance Training Group Det, NAS North Island San Diego CA	1

09/07/2002

** PRIVACY ACT INFORMATION **

INFORMATION NOT INCLUDED ON THE SMART

The SMART does not include information about college courses taken by sailors or marines before they entered active duty. SMART also does not include data about basic training for sailors who entered active duty before 1 April 1979 or data about basic training for marines who entered active duty before 1976. These are the dates that ACE first evaluated the training. ACE does recommend, however, that colleges award credit for or waive the requirement for physical education and hygiene for any servicemember with at least six months of military service, regardless of whether that servicemember received a specific credit recommendation for basic training.

Additionally, course attendance dates are not available for courses taken by marines prior to 1994. As a result, resident courses prior to 1994 may appear in the "other learning experiences" section of the SMART. Credit may be awarded by providing documentation of the attendance dates to the evaluating academic institution.

OBTAINING A COPY OF YOUR SMART

The SMART service is free. To request a personal, unofficial SMART, you can call, fax, e-mail, or mail the Navy College Center at the Naval Education and Training Professional Development and Technology Center (NET-PDTC): NETPDTC N2A5, 6490 Saufley Field Road, Pensacola, FL 32509-5204. The toll-free telephone number is DSN 922-1828 or (877) 253-7122, and the commercial toll number is (850) 452-1828; the fax number is DSN 922-1281 or (850) 452-1281 (commercial); and the e-mail address is *ncc@smtp.cnet.navy.mil*. Hours are from 0600 (6 A.M.) to 2100 (9 P.M.) central standard time, seven days a week, except Thanksgiving, Christmas, New Year's, and the Fourth of July. The request should include your name, social security number, date of birth, and mailing address. The Navy College Center will mail the unofficial transcript to you. You also can order an unofficial copy of your SMART at your local Navy College Office or Marine Corps Education Center; some locations can provide you with an unofficial, but locally printed copy of the transcript. Remember that colleges will not accept transcripts directly from the servicemember as official. To request an official copy, which is mailed directly to the college or university you designate, you should obtain a SMART Request Form from your local Navy College Office or Marine Corps Education Center, and mail or fax it to the address or fax number on the form. Upon receipt of the form, the Navy College Center will mail the official transcript to the college or colleges designated. You also can submit the form in person to the local Navy College Office or Marine Corps Education Center.

For more information, see the Navy College Center website: *www.navycollege.navy.mil.*

MAKING CORRECTIONS TO SMART

Each SMART comes with an attached form that explains how to make corrections. If your course data need to be changed due to an improper database entry at the Navy schoolhouse, you should provide a copy of your course completion certificate or page 4 from your service record to the Navy College Center. The personnel support detachment (PSD) must stamp "Certified as a True Copy" and sign the course certificate on page 4 before you submit it. You should keep in mind that the training activity where you took the course may have changed its name. If the command's unit identification code (UIC) remained the same, the SMART will list the latest command name. For Navy members, the rank displayed is the rank received from master data file (MDF) at Navy Personnel Command (NPC). Until a new rank is officially in the MDF, it will not appear on the SMART. If the MDF has not been updated, you should contact your PSD or personnel and administrative office to have corrections made and sent to the Navy Personnel Command. It will normally take at least thirty business days before the SMART is corrected.

COLLEGE ACCEPTANCE OF THE SMART CREDIT RECOMMENDATIONS

Academic institutions establish their own policies on credit transfers. The amount of credit awarded will depend on your school's policy and your degree program. However, Servicemembers Opportunity Colleges Navy (SOCNAV) and Servicemembers Opportunity Colleges Marine Corps (SOCMAR) are generally more flexible when evaluating military experiences for credit toward a degree. Also, military training evaluated by ACE can be accepted by a college either before or after you have separated from the Navy or Marine Corps.

6

Navy College Program

The Navy College Program (NCP) is a voluntary education program designed to meet the educational needs of sailors and, to a lesser extent, marines. The goal of NCP is to provide sailors with an uncomplicated way to pursue a degree no matter where they serve. Participation is voluntary. Sailors can decide to participate when they are ready and at their own pace. The NCP provides sailors with opportunities for college degrees by providing academic credit for Navy training, work experience, and off-duty education. NCP is primarily geared toward enlisted sailors. However, some NCP components are also available to officers. Besides the SMART, which was discussed in the previous chapter, the primary components of the NCP are rating and degree road maps and the Navy College rating partner schools, Servicemembers Opportunity Colleges Navy (SOCNAV), the Navy College Program for Afloat College Education (NCPACE), the Academic Skills Program, and academic advice.

NAVY COLLEGE RATING PARTNERS
In responding to sailors' need for greater access to higher education, the Navy College Program (NCP) developed partnerships with colleges and universities to offer rating-related degrees via distance learning so that sailors anywhere could pursue a degree. These education partnerships provide associate and bachelor's degree programs related to each rating and make maximum use of military professional training and experience to fulfill degree requirements. The goal of the Navy College Rating Partner Schools is to support both the mobile lifestyle and educational goals of sailors with rate-related degree programs. Courses are offered in a variety of formats, such as CD-ROM, videotape, paper, or online. Contact your Navy College Office or the Navy College Center about degree programs available from your partnership schools.

Rating and Degree Road Maps

Rating road maps identify ACE-recommended college credit for Navy training and rating-specific work experience across a Navy career. Degree road maps are rate-related degrees that make the most of recommended credit for Navy training and on-the-job experience. The Navy has partnerships with colleges and universities that offer degrees through distance learning for all enlisted ratings.

Schools Participating in the NCP as Rating Partners

The following colleges and universities participate as NCP rating partners and offer degree programs in the corresponding ratings:

City University
JO, PH

Coastline Community College of California
AT, BU, CM, CTM, DT, EA, EM(NUC), EN, EO, ET(NUC), GSE, GSM, HM, HT, MM, MM(NUC), MM(SUB), MR, SW, UT

Dallas Telecollege of the Dallas Community Colleges
YN

Embry-Riddle Aeronautical University
ABE, ABF, ABH, AC, AD, AE, AG, AME, AMH, AMS, AO, AS, AT, AW, PR

Empire State College
ABF, ABH, AK, AMH, AMS, CTR, CTT, DC, DK, ET, FC, GM, HT, IS, IT, MN, MS, OS, SH, SK, TM

Florida Community College at Jacksonville
All Navy enlisted rates

Florida State University
All Navy enlisted rates

Fort Hays State University
AZ, BM, CTA, CTM, CTO, CTR, CTT, ET, EW, FC, GM, IC, IT, MA, MN, NC, PC, PN, QM, RP, SM, TM, YN

George Washington University
HM(IDC)

Old Dominion University
ABE, AE, AT, CTM, CTR, CTT, DT, EM, EM(NUC), EN, ET,
  ET(NUC), FC, FT, GM, GSE, GSM, HM, MM, MM(NUC),
  MM(SUB), MR, MT, STG, STS

Pikes Peak Community College
MA

Rogers State University
AT, EM, ET(NUC), EW, FC, MM(NUC), MM(SUB), STG

Thomas Edison State College
AC, AD, AE, AG, BU, CE, CM, CTI, CTM, DT, EM, EM(NUC), ET,
  ET(NUC), EW, FT, GM, GSE, IC, MM(NUC), MM(SUB), MT,
  MU, PH, RP

Troy State University
AK, CTA, DK, SK

University of Maryland University College
BM, CTO, DM, FT, IS, IT, LN, OS, QM, SM, YN

Vincennes University
AZ, ET, IC, LI, MA, PC, PN, STG, STS, YN

SOCNAV

Servicemembers Opportunity Colleges Navy (SOCNAV) consists of a network of accredited colleges offering specific associate and bachelor's degrees to Navy members worldwide through resident courses or distance learning. Colleges taking part in each curriculum area guarantee to accept each other's credits for transfer, so students do not lose credits. Many SOCNAV networks are closely related to Navy ratings, resulting in maximum award of credit for Navy training. The "home" college issues an official evaluation of all prior learning on a SOCNAV agreement. This agreement serves as the student's long-range degree plan. SOCNAV colleges offer degrees in many different areas. SOCNAV colleges all over the world can be used to satisfy the degree requirements of the home college. SOCNAV programs are available at many military installations; distance learning options are available everywhere. The SOCNAV degree plan prevents the student from duplicating courses already completed. Required residency is kept to a minimum. Additional information, including a complete list of all Servicemembers Opportunity Colleges, is provided in chapter 15. Further information on SOCNAV is available at the Servicemembers Opportunity Colleges website: *www.soc.aascu.org*.

NAVY COLLEGE PROGRAM FOR AFLOAT COLLEGE EDUCATION

The Navy College Program for Afloat College Education (NCPACE) offers instruction in both academic skills and college (undergraduate and graduate) courses. All NCPACE college courses are provided by regionally accredited colleges and universities. NCPACE provides sailors the opportunity to continue their education while on sea duty assignments such as on a ship or at a remote site. Courses are taught using technology such as computers and video teleconferencing and by traditional classroom instruction. All undergraduate courses are offered by Servicemembers Opportunity Colleges in order to allow sailors the opportunity to transfer credits and complete degrees.

NCPACE Eligibility

Eligibility for NCPACE courses depends on military assignment. Naval personnel assigned or attached to ships, whether deployed, pier side, or in the shipyard, may take instructor-delivered and technology-delivered NCPACE courses on a continuous basis. All instructor-delivered courses are taught aboard ship, barge, or floating dry dock.

Naval personnel assigned to shore commands, precommissioning units, and air squadrons with sea duty UICs, types 2, 3, 4, and 8, may take technology-delivered NCPACE courses on a continuous basis. They may participate in courses delivered by an instructor aboard ships only if their schedule and time permit them to complete the course.

Naval personnel assigned to geographically remote sites as specified in the NCPACE contract may take technology-delivered NCPACE courses on a continuous basis.

Naval personnel assigned to ships in a decommissioning status may continue all NCPACE services as long as there are sufficient crew members on board to support the minimum enrollments established in the contract.

Marines who are part of the ship's company have access to all NCPACE services. Marines who are embarked on Navy ships, but are not part of the ship's company, may participate in shipboard instructor-delivered courses (no computer-delivered courses) on a space-available basis. This means that the minimum course enrollment (ten sailors) has been met for each course ordered by the ship.

Courses Offered by NCPACE

NCPACE offers instructor-taught college courses in the following subjects: accounting, anthropology, art, biology, business, communications, computer science, economics, English, geography, history, Japanese, law enforcement, mathematics, management, microcomputer technology, philosophy, physical sciences, political science, psychology, real estate, sociology, Spanish, and speech.

NCPACE offers technology-delivered college courses in the following subjects: astronomy, business, computer science, economics, education, English, French, geology, history, humanities, information systems management, management, mathematics, philosophy, physics, political science, psychology, sociology, and Spanish.

ACADEMIC SKILLS PROGRAM

The Academic Skills Program provides the educational foundation for the Navy College Program. To assist in preparation for college courses, the Navy provides instruction in basic subjects. Sailors may work on English, mathematics, and reading skills ashore either at the Navy College Learning Center (NCLC) computer labs or in the Navy College Learning Program (NCLP) instructor-taught classes. In either program, sailors are given diagnostic tests and begin instruction at a level appropriate to their needs. Instruction in academic skills is available at no cost to sailors or their command. If sailors are assigned to a sea duty command, free instruction is available through NCPACE. At the NCLCs, sailors may also work in the following subjects: algebra, calculus, geometry, trigonometry, chemistry, physics, science, social studies, life and job skills, and parenting skills. Also, test preparations for the Armed Services Vocational Aptitude Battery (ASVAB), GED, SAT, and CLEP examinations are available.

With NCLP students may enroll in as many classes as they can fit into their work and personal schedules. Each NCLP class is held for a total of forty-five hours. Classes are usually scheduled over a period of three to eight weeks. Instruction in the classes is limited to no more than four hours each day. Students are given a placement test on the first day of class. Depending on the results of the placement test, the instructor will prepare the NCLP course materials to meet the student's needs. During one of the last classes, students are given a test to see how much they have progressed. Students receive a certificate for successfully completing the class if their test score is equal to or greater than their placement test score and if they have attended at least 80 percent of the classes.

NCLC and NCLP Academic Skills Program Eligibility
All active-duty military personnel of all services assigned to the base supporting the NCLC are eligible to use the NCLC Academic Skills Program. Also, in order of priority, active-duty Navy personnel with shore duty UICs, active-duty Navy personnel with sea duty UICs, and adults with valid U.S. military identification may also use the NCLC Academic Skills Program.

In order of priority, all active-duty Navy personnel with shore duty UICs, all active-duty Navy personnel with sea duty UICs, active-duty marines assigned to the base or tenant command hosting the class, active-duty personnel from other services, and other Department of Defense personnel may enroll in NCLP classes.

ACADEMIC ADVICE
The best source of academic advice is the professionals at the Navy College Office. If you prefer, you can seek advice and ask questions from academic advisors at the Navy College Center (NCC). The NCC serves as the Navy College Program's central location for receiving and responding to toll-free telephone, e-mail, fax, and postal inquiries dealing with all off-duty voluntary education programs and services. The NCC also serves as a hub for requesting the SMART. It provides easy access to and "one-stop shopping" for information on the NCP and existing voluntary education opportunities.

The NCC is open between 0600 (6 A.M.) and 2100 (9 P.M.) hours, seven days a week (except Christmas, New Year's, Thanksgiving, and the Fourth of July). The NCC can be contacted by mail, phone, fax, or e-mail. The NCC's address is Commanding Officer, Naval Education and Training Professional Development and Technology Center, Navy College Center, Code N2A5, 6490 Saufley Field Road, Pensacola, FL 32509-5204. The toll-free number is (877) 253-7122 or DSN 922-1828; the fax number is DSN 922-1281 or (850) 452-1281 (commercial); and the e-mail address is *ncc@smtp.cnet.navy.mil*. Navy personnel overseas also can contact the NCC using the following toll-free numbers:

Australia	1-800-1-27961
Belgium	0800-76961
France	0800-900640

Germany	195-049-8877
Greece	00800-12-5281
Italy	800-874858
Japan	00531-120097
Korea	00798-14-800-4441
Luxembourg	8002-9142
Mexico	001-8772537122
Philippines	102-71800-120-1501
Portugal	8008-12461
Singapore	800-1203426
Spain	900-931932
Taiwan	0080-13-9821
Thailand	001-800-12-0663329
United Kingdom	08-001698252

More information about the Navy College Program can be found at the NCP website: *www.navycollege.navy.mil.*

NAVAL POSTGRADUATE SCHOOL

Although not officially part of the NCP, the Naval Postgraduate School in Monterey, California, offers a number of degrees for officers, including a defense-focused Master of Business Administration (MBA) degree. The program covers all elements of a typical MBA program, but focuses some of the material on military-specific issues. Attendance is by service application and selection, like a typical college.

Military officers, primarily in the O-3 and O-4 grades, attend the school for eighteen months on a resident basis. Most officers are from the Navy, but officers from other services and civilians are welcome to apply. The first fifty students begin the program in January, and another 100 begin studies in the summer. New classes start twice a year.

The MBA program has three pieces. A business core will reflect subjects covered in other MBA programs, albeit with a defense focus. Subjects might include economics for a defense manager and an organizational design course focused on defense organizations. The second piece consists of mission-related coursework. This might be aimed at defense management, resource determination, e-business for defense, and the defense budget and appropriations process. The third piece consists of individual concentration courses geared to specific assignments, which might be acquisition and contracting, logistics, financial management, personnel management, or information management.

In September 2002, the school entered into a partnership with the University of Maryland to offer the same degree on a nonresident basis in Washington, D.C. Classes will meet on Saturdays with common subjects to be taught by Maryland professors and military-specific subjects to be taught by visiting faculty from Monterey or through distance-learning methods.

Individuals seeking more information on this program should see their personnel managers or check the school's website at *www.nps.navy.mil.*

7

Marine Corps
Lifelong Learning

Lifelong Learning is a series of Marine Corps educational programs designed to help marines and their family members meet their educational needs. Among the programs included in Lifelong Learning are the Afloat Education Program, the United Services Military Apprenticeship Program, the Marine Corps Satellite Education Network, the Military Academic Skills Program, Servicemembers Opportunity Colleges Marine Corps (SOCMAR), and the Sailor/Marine American Council on Education Registry Transcript, which was covered in chapter 5.

AFLOAT EDUCATION PROGRAM
The purpose of the Marine Corps afloat program is to provide college courses to afloat marines. The Navy College Program for Afloat College Education (NCPACE), under a Navy contract, offers instruction in both academic skills and college (undergraduate and graduate) courses to sailors and embarked marines. Currently under NCPACE, marines participate on a space-available basis unless they are a ship's company marines. The Navy pays the cost. College and academic skills courses are delivered aboard ship using technology such as computers and video teleconferencing and traditional classroom instruction if berthing space permits. Tuition assistance for servicemembers enrolled in NCPACE courses is paid at a rate of 100 percent as allowed by Title 10, U.S. Code, Section 2007. The servicemember is responsible for registration and book fees. For more details, see a full description of NCPACE in the previous chapter.

UNITED SERVICES MILITARY APPRENTICESHIP PROGRAM
The United Services Military Apprenticeship Program (USMAP) is a consolidated apprenticeship program that includes the Navy, the Marine Corps,

and the Coast Guard. USMAP provides apprenticeship training in 107 occupations and is the largest apprenticeship program sponsor registered with the U.S. Department of Labor. USMAP eliminates work duplication through individually registered apprenticeship programs and provides apprenticeship training that will help military personnel qualify for employment in a recognized civilian trade after the expiration of their enlistment. From an educational perspective, USMAP promotes the recognition of the value of military personnel training and experience through the issuance of a certificate of completion from the U.S. Department of Labor.

MOS Eligible for USMAP

The following list shows the military occupational specialties (MOSs), required hours of experience, and required hours of related instruction needed for apprenticeship:

Aims symbol	Occupational title	Required hours	Required instructional hours
0005M	Aircraft/airframe power plant mechanic	8000	576
0880M	Audio-video repairer	4000	288
0023M	Automobile mechanic	8000	576
0863M	Aviation ordnanceman (aircraft armament mechanic)	8000	576
0320M	Aviation structural mechanic	8000	576
0950M	Bulk fuel specialist (pumper-gauger)	6000	432
0067M	Carpenter (combat engineer)	8000	576
0077M	Central office repairer	8000	576
0663M	Cook (hotel and restaurant)	6000	432
0159M	Electrician	8000	576
0643M	Electrician, maintenance	8000	576
0170M	Electronics mechanic	8000	576
0336M	Engineer equipment mechanic (construction)	8000	576
0110M	Graphic designer	3000	216
0980M	Heavy vehicle operator (truck driver)	3500	252
0800M	Legal secretary	2200	158
0361M	Lithographer (off-set press operator)	8000	576
0296M	Machinist-M	8000	576
0372M	Ordnance artificer (artillery repair technician)	6000	432

0372M	Ordnance artificer (turret repairer)	6000	432
0955M	Photographer, motion picture	6000	432
0403M	Photographer, still	6000	432
0432M	Plumber	8000	576
0948M	Purchasing agent	8000	576
0465M	Radio mechanic	6000	432
0666M	Refrigeration mechanic	6000	432
0551M	Surveyor assistant	4000	288
0001M	Weather observer	4000	288
0622M	Welder, combination	6000	432

Signing Up for USMAP

Marines must first complete an Apprentice Registration Application (CNET Form 1560/1). Applications can be obtained from the local educational services office, training office, command career counselor, Marine Lifelong Learning Center, or USMAP office. When you complete your application, send it, along with documentation showing the U.S. Marine Corps (USMC) schools you attended and the date you earned your MOS to the USMAP office. Designated personnel E-1 through E-9 are eligible for the program if qualified. The USMAP needs your advancement date to E-4 in order to award you all the preregistration credit you deserve. When the USMAP office receives your application, it will review it. If all information is correct, the application will be processed and registered with the Department of Labor, Bureau of Apprenticeship and Training, Washington, D.C. Your application will then be returned to you. After receiving your approved Apprenticeship Registration Application, you can obtain your Work Experience Hourly Records and the Work Processes Schedule for your trade by printing them from the USMAP home page. If information is missing on your application or qualifications are not met, your application package will be returned to you, via your commanding officer, for corrections.

MARINE CORPS SATELLITE EDUCATION NETWORK

The Marine Corps Satellite Education Network (MCSEN) is a network of video teleconferencing systems located on Marine Corps installations throughout the United States and Japan that are used to enhance educational opportunities offered to marines. The objective of MCSEN is to transform the Marine Corps worldwide network of education centers into one worldwide college campus. MCSEN makes higher education more accessible than it has ever been to the thousands of marines stationed around the world. This two-way communication system enables marines to matriculate in similar degree programs regardless of duty station. Professors are able to teach courses to marines thousands of miles away, and students will be able to interact from distant classrooms in "real time" utilizing color monitors, graphic presentations, and microphones.

MCSEN Degree Programs and Schools
The Associate of Arts in Paralegal Studies, Associate of Science in Criminal Justice, and Associate of Science in General Studies degree programs are offered via the MCSEN system. These programs are offered by Hinds Community College and Coastline Community College. For more information about either of these schools, visit their websites: *www.hinds.cc.ms.us/mcsen* (Hinds Community College) or *www.marine.ccc.cccd.edu* (Coastline Community College).

MCSEN System Locations
The MCSEN systems are available at the following locations:
Commanding General TEECG, 29 Palms, California
Headquarters U.S. Marine Corps, Henderson Hall, Arlington, Virginia
Marine Air Ground Task Force Training Command, 29 Palms, California
Marine Corps Air Station, Beaufort, South Carolina
Marine Corps Air Station, Cherry Point, North Carolina
Marine Corps Air Station, Iwakuni, Japan
Marine Corps Air Station, Miramar, San Diego, California
Marine Corps Air Station, Yuma, Arizona
Marine Corps Base, Camp Butler, Okinawa, Japan
Marine Corps Base, Camp Lejeune, North Carolina
Marine Corps Base, Camp Pendleton, California
Marine Corps Base, Kaneohe Bay, Hawaii
Marine Corps Combat Development Command, Quantico, Virginia
Marine Corps Logistics Base, Albany, Georgia
Marine Corps Logistics Base, Barstow, California
Marine Corps Recruit Depot, Parris Island, South Carolina
Marine Corps Recruit Depot, San Diego, California

MILITARY ACADEMIC SKILLS PROGRAM
The Military Academic Skills Program (MASP) was developed to improve the competencies of active-duty enlisted personnel in the academic skills of reading, communication/writing, and mathematics.

MASP is targeted toward enlisted personnel with a general technical (GT) score of 99 or below or enlisted personnel who score below 10.2 on the Test for Adult Basic Education (TABE). Individuals may be referred by their commanding officers to improve work performance and may refer themselves for career, professional, and personal development.

MASP may be delivered over MCSEN, by traditional classroom (at the commander's request), by online classroom, or by an afloat classroom (at the commander's request).

SOCMAR

Servicemembers Opportunity Colleges Marine Corps (SOCMAR) is a network of colleges and universities established to assist marines in earning a college degree through resident courses or distance learning. Colleges taking part in each curriculum area guarantee to accept each other's credits for transfer, so students do not lose credits. The "home" college issues an official evaluation of all prior learning on a SOCMAR agreement. This agreement serves as the student's long-range degree plan. SOCMAR colleges offer degrees in many different areas. The SOCMAR degree plan prevents the student from duplicating courses already completed. Required residency is kept to a minimum. Additional information, including a complete list of all Servicemembers Opportunity Colleges, is provided in chapter 15. Further information on SOCMAR is available at Servicemembers Opportunity Colleges website: *www.soc.aascu.org*.

PART IV

AIR FORCE PROGRAMS

8

Community College
of the Air Force

The Community College of the Air Force (CCAF) is the only degree-granting institution of higher learning in the world dedicated exclusively to enlisted people. CCAF was activated in 1972, and in 1977 the college was certified with degree-granting authority. Since awarding its first Associate of Applied Science degree in 1977, the college has awarded over 200,000 degrees.

Today it is the largest multicampus community college in the world and is the only community college in the Department of Defense. CCAF offers enlisted members of the active-duty Air Force, Air National Guard, and Air Force Reserve Command the opportunity to earn two-year Associate of Applied Science degrees directly related to their Air Force Specialty Codes (AFSCs).

CCAF is fully accredited by the Commission on Colleges of the Southern Association of Colleges and Schools to award the Associate of Applied Science degree.

PURPOSE AND IMPORTANCE OF CCAF

The purpose of CCAF is to qualify airmen for an Associate of Applied Science (AAS) degree in their AFSC by combining Air Force technical training, off-duty education at civilian schools and colleges, and professional military education.

CCAF is important because it allows you to consolidate your military and civilian education in a single system and earn a college degree that is recognized throughout the military and civilian communities. With CCAF you can obtain college credit for your military technical schools, choose an educational path that allows you to apply your knowledge, improve your chances of promotion, and better prepare yourself for life after the military.

HOW DOES CCAF COMPARE TO CIVILIAN COLLEGES?

CCAF is certainly not the typical civilian college. Because the organization and administration of CCAF is designed to meet the unique needs of Air Force enlisted personnel, it is often perceived as a nontraditional college. Being nontraditional, however, does not mean that CCAF has lower standards than its civilian counterparts. In fact, the standards for an associate degree at CCAF exceed those at many civilian community colleges. By combining the latest Air Force technical training with course work from civilian colleges to satisfy the degree requirements, CCAF has earned a well-deserved reputation as a highly effective educational institution.

ENROLLMENT IN CCAF

Air Force enlisted personnel are automatically registered into the degree program applicable to their AFSC and awarded 4 semester hours of credit when they graduate from basic military training. Air Force personnel can continue to earn college credit as they complete entry-level, advanced, and skill-upgrade technical training and courses at the Airman Leadership School, the NCO Academy, and the Senior NCO Academy.

Although soldiers, sailors, and marines may complete some individual courses granted credit by the CCAF and may request transcripts, only enlisted members of the Air Force, Air National Guard, and Air Force Reserve Command may enroll in a degree program.

Prior to enlistment in the Air Force, individuals must complete the Armed Services Vocational Aptitude Battery (ASVAB), meeting the standards specified in AETC Instruction 36-2002, *Recruiting Procedures for the Air Force.* Composite scores of the ASVAB indicate academic and career field aptitude. Scores are used to counsel individuals and place them in Air Force career areas that match their aptitudes and abilities. The college uses these scores as an indicator of the student's potential to make satisfactory progress in a career-related degree program.

Upon assignment to an Air Force career field, active-duty, Air National Guard, and Air Force Reserve Command enlisted members are admitted to the college and registered in the degree program for their AFSC as nonparticipants. Their registration status does not change until they receive formal academic advisement and provide official transcripts from a regionally accredited institution reflecting completion of civilian college course work or national tests applicable to their degree program. At the formal advisement session, the student must declare all institutions attended so course credit can be considered for acceptance in transfer if applicable to a degree program. Once a civilian college course or national test is posted to a record, the student is identified as an active participant.

CCAF DEGREE PROGRAMS AND REQUIREMENTS

Individuals may participate in degree programs designed for their Air Force occupation in one of five general areas: logistics and resources, public and support services, allied health, electronics and telecommunications, and aircraft and missile maintenance.

CCAF offers sixty-six different degree programs:

Aerospace ground equipment technology
Aerospace historian
Aerospace physiology technology
Air and space operations technology
Aircraft armament systems technology
Aircrew life support
Airport resource management
Airway science
Allied health sciences
Audiovisual production services
Aviation maintenance
Aviation operations
Avionic systems technology
Bioenvironmental engineering technology
Biomedical equipment technology
Cardiopulmonary laboratory technology
Communications application technology
Computer science technology
Construction technology
Contracts management
Criminal justice
Dental assisting
Dental laboratory technology
Disaster preparedness
Ecological controls
Education and training management
Electronic systems technology
Explosive ordnance disposal
Fabrication and parachute technology
Financial management
Fire science
Fitness, recreations, and services management
Food and nutritional science
Healthcare management
Histologic technology

Information management
Information systems technology
Instructor of technology and military science
Logistics
Maintenance production management
Mechanical and electrical technology
Medical laboratory technology
Mental health services
Metals technology
Missile and space systems maintenance
Munitions systems technology
Music
Nondestructive testing technology
Nuclear medicine technology
Optometric technician
Paralegal
Pararescue
Personnel administration
Pharmacy technology
Physical therapist assistant
Public affairs
Public health technology
Radiologic technology
Safety
Scientific analysis technology
Social services
Surgical services technology
Survival instructor
Transportation
Vehicle maintenance
Weather technology

Each degree program consists of 64 semester hours (SH) and combines Air Force education and training with a core of general education requirements obtained from civilian education sources. The 64 semester hours must be earned in the following areas:

- Physical education (4 SH): satisfied by completing basic training.
- Technical education (24 SH): satisfied by completing entry-level and advanced technical courses and skill-level upgrades or by applicable civilian course work, credit by examination, or certification/licensure.

- General education (15 SH): consists of oral communications (3 SH), written communications (3 SH), mathematics (3 SH), social science (3 SH), and humanities (3 SH). Satisfied by application of the following course work accepted in transfer from regionally accredited institutions or through testing.
- Leadership, management, and military studies (LMMS) (6 SH): satisfied by attendance at Airman Leadership School, NCO Academy, or the Air Force Senior NCO Academy or by completion of civilian courses that emphasize fundamentals of management or management of human resources.
- Program electives (15 SH): satisfied by credit from either general education, LMMS, or technical education.

Students must have a minimum of 16 semester hours of CCAF credit applied to their degree program in order to graduate.

WHAT QUALIFIES FOR CREDIT AT CCAF?

CCAF may award college credit for completion of 3, 5, and 7 skill-level training, attainment of 9 skill level, completion of Senior NCO Academy courses, completion of correspondence or residence courses at major command NCO Academy courses, completion of most leadership schools, and basic training (physical education credit). Credit also may be awarded for many formal Air Force technical schools, courses from accredited colleges or universities, correspondence courses from any accredited college or university, and college-level tests such as CLEP and DANTES exams.

CCAF students can apply a maximum of 30 semester hours of credit toward their degree from college-level tests such as the CLEP general exam, CLEP subject exam, DANTES subject exams, and exams from Excelsior College (formerly Regents College). Students may also earn credit for the Defense Language Proficiency Test.

Credit may be awarded to students who successfully complete a degree-applicable equivalency examination administered by an affiliated school. Only program-applicable equivalency examination credit will be transcribed.

Degree requirements may be satisfied upon verification of degree-relevant governmental and/or professional certification, licensure, or registry. Students who hold a degree-relevant certification, licensure, or registry must contact the sponsoring agency, association, or society and request that an official written verification be sent to CCAF/RRR, 130 West Maxwell Boulevard, Maxwell AFB, AL 36112-6613.

Many Air Force enlisted members attend Army, Navy, and Department of Defense initial advanced technical training courses instead of Air Force technical training courses. Since these technical training schools are not part of the CCAF system, the college does not award resident credit for the courses. However, the college does award proficiency credit to Air Force enlisted members who complete these courses and demonstrate apprentice-level competency. Proficiency credit is applied to a student's program upon attainment of the journeyman, 5 skill level. Proficiency credit does not apply to the residency requirement. The 16-semester-hour residency requirement can be satisfied only by credit earned in an affiliated school or through internship credit awarded for progression in an Air Force occupational specialty. If the other service school is accredited and issues a transcript, the college will consider accepting the credit in transfer. Courses recommended for credit in the *Guide to the Evaluation of Educational Experiences in the Armed Services* may be applied to a CCAF degree.

Some of the courses that do not qualify for CCAF credit include traffic safety training, small-arms marksmanship training, base-level management courses, and Air Force Extension Course Institute (ECI) courses. However, the Senior NCO Academy, major command NCO Academy, and some of the specialized courses do qualify for CCAF credit.

DEGREE COMPLETION REQUIREMENTS

Students enrolled in the instructor of technology and military science program have two years from date of registration to complete their degree. Students enrolled in all other programs have six years from date of registration to complete their degree. Students who are pursuing their first CCAF degree and do not complete it in the allotted time will automatically be moved to the degree program for their primary occupational specialty in the most current catalog. They will be required to meet the requirements of the current catalog. Students who are pursuing a subsequent CCAF degree are disenrolled at the end of the allotted time if they have not completed it. However, they may reregister in a subsequent degree program by submitting Air Force Form 968, *Community College of the Air Force Action Request*, through their education services office or Air National Guard or Air Force Reserve Command CCAF advisor.

In order to graduate, students must hold a journeyman (5) level at the time of program completion and have a minimum of 16 semester hours of CCAF credit applied to their degree program.

Airmen may register in a subsequent degree program for which they have a primary AFSC or second, third, or fourth (not duty or control) AFSC, provided they have not been awarded a degree in a program designed for that career field. CCAF degree holders who register in another program must earn and have applied a minimum of 24 semester hours of unique (different) technical credit, 12 semester hours of which must be CCAF credit.

Since participation in a degree program is voluntary, students may formally request withdrawal from the program in which they are registered. Students requesting this action must complete and sign Air Force Form 968 and forward it to the CCAF registrar at CCAF/RR, 130 West Maxwell Boulevard, Maxwell AFB, AL 36112-6613.

AIR FORCE-INSTRUCTED COLLEGE CREDIT FOR SOLDIERS, SAILORS, AND MARINES

Many of the official courses and training taught under the authority of the Air Force are affiliated with the Community College of the Air Force, which awards college credit for many military training experiences. Many of these Air Force courses are offered to personnel of the other services. If you are not sure whether an Air Force-instructed course you attended is awarded credit, request a transcript from the CCAF.

For more information, see the CCAF's website: *www.au.af.mil/au/ccaf.*

9

Beyond CCAF

While many enlisted members of the Air Force, Air National Guard, and Air Force Reserve take advantage of the opportunity to earn an Associate in Applied Science degree with the Community College of the Air Force, they are sometimes left mystified about the best path to completing their bachelor's degree and beyond. Where Air Force personnel used the formulated plans of CCAF to pursue a two-year degree in a field directly related to their AFSCs, they now have several choices of programs and services from which to choose when selecting and pursuing a bachelor's or master's degree.

All the nontraditional education programs listed in Part V of this book are available to Air Force personnel wishing to pursue associate degrees, or bachelor's and master's degrees.

Some of these most popular programs are the Servicemembers Opportunity Colleges Program and DANTES Distance Learning Programs. These programs are often recommended for Air Force personnel who have earned their associate's degree from the CCAF and who wish to continue their educational development by pursuing a four-year degree or graduate study.

SERVICEMEMBER OPPORTUNITY COLLEGES
Servicemember Opportunity Colleges are colleges and universities that have developed special policies and procedures for military personnel that make it easier for them to earn college degrees. There are over 1,500 colleges that participate in the Servicemembers Opportunity Colleges Program and all offer special policies and procedures to their military college students pursuing degrees. Like CCAF, these civilian schools grant college credit for military training. They also recognize knowledge gained through nontraditional methods and minimize the residency requirements for military personnel. Air Force education personnel offer professional counseling to help guide

Air Force personnel in selecting the appropriate schools and programs. The Servicemember Opportunity Colleges Program is discussed in detail in chapter 15.

DANTES DISTANCE LEARNING PROGRAMS
There are actually three different programs available: the Independent Study Program, the DANTES External Degree Program, and the DANTES Nationally Accredited Distance Learning Program.

The DANTES *Independent Study* Program allows servicemembers to select and complete individual college courses at the undergraduate and graduate levels from regionally accredited institutions.

The DANTES *External Degree* Program provides degree programs from regionally accredited colleges and universities that have few or no residency requirements for degree completion. With this program, Air Force members can pursue a variety of bachelor's and master's degrees. The DANTES External Degree Catalog includes information for approximately 225 baccalaureate and 100 graduate degree programs.

The DANTES *Nationally Accredited Distance Learning* Program provides an opportunity for military personnel to take vocational, technical, and some nontechnical courses to earn bachelor's and master's degrees in vocational programs.

Using these programs, servicemembers can complete college, technical, and vocational courses from accredited U.S. colleges and universities using everything from traditional textbooks to computer networks to video conferencing. Air Force personnel can take a single course or complete entire bachelor's and master's degrees, most with little or no classroom attendance.

Participating Schools
Schools ranging from the University of Alabama to the University of Wyoming and from Embry-Riddle Aeronautical University to Penn State University participate in the DANTES programs. A complete list of schools that participate in these programs, along with more details, is included in chapter 12.

AIR FORCE INSTITUTE FOR ADVANCED DISTRIBUTED LEARNING
In addition to Servicemember Opportunity Colleges and DANTES distance learning programs, the Air Force has the Air Force Institute for Advanced Distributed Learning, a program that can be used to facilitate completion of undergraduate degrees by both resident and nonresident methods.

The Air Force Institute for Advanced Distributed Learning (AFIADL) is the new name for the Air Force's Extension Course Institute (ECI). The ECI was originally established in 1950 as a professional specialized school of the Air University. As a correspondence school, the ECI's original mission was to provide voluntary nonresident courses for both active-duty and reserve Air Force personnel.

Today, the AFIADL has a reputation for continued excellence in correspondence education. With accreditation through the Distance Education and Training Council and review by the Air University Board of Visitors, the AFIADL now offers formal training and educational programs for Air Force, Air National Guard, Air Force Reserve, the Department of Defense, and other federal agencies.

The Air Force Institute for Advanced Distributed Learning's entire focus is distance learning, and it delivers education and training at a distance by developing, publishing and distributing career development courses, professional military education and specialized courses to Air Force personnel throughout the world.

Does AFIADL Help Complete a Bachelor's Degree?

Many AFIADL courses have been evaluated by the American Council on Education and are recommended for college credit in upper-division baccalaureate, lower-division baccalaureate, and vocational areas. These recommendations allow many AFIADL courses to be included in undergraduate degree programs to assist Air Force personnel in satisfying the requirements for their bachelor's degrees at servicemember opportunity colleges.

AFIADL also operates in a fully automated environment. Course development, production, distribution, and the registrar and student administration functions are managed on an advanced system consisting of hundreds of computers.

Courses Offered by AFIADL

AFIADL offers over 400 nonresident courses in three categories: professional military education courses, specialized courses, and career development courses.

Many Air Force personnel are familiar with AFIADL's professional military education (PME) courses. The courses are taken by both commissioned and noncommissioned officers, and they teach leadership, management principles, techniques of effective communication, problem solving, analysis of professional reading materials, international relations, national decision making, and defense management. These courses also cover topics such as the psychology of learning, individual differences, and the techniques of teaching. The courses give students the broad skills and knowledge needed to be effective at various stages in their careers. Some PME instruction also is available by correspondence, seminar, or in-residence through the subject schools. Some of the PME courses offered by AFIADL include the Noncommissioned Officer Academy Correspondence Course, the Airmen Leadership School Associate Program, the Senior Noncommissioned Officer Academy Correspondence Course, and the Senior Noncommissioned Officer Academy Multimedia Correspondence Course.

AFIADL specialized courses provide valuable information and career broadening knowledge to Air Force personnel. AFIADL offers specialized courses in several career fields.

Course Title	Course Field Number
Aircrew Operations	(1A)
Weather	(1W)
General Military Training	(12)
Supervisor Safety	(19)
Public Affairs (CAP)	(20)
Safety (CAP)	(21)
Mission Support	(3S)
Communications-Electronics	(30)
Medical	(4B)
Nursing	(46)
Civil Engineering	(55)
Logistics, Plans and Programs	(66)
Financial	(67)
Personnel	(73)
Public Affairs	(79)
Security Police	(81)

Much of the AFIADL's curriculum is comprised of career development courses (CDCs). These self-study courses help enlisted personnel obtain specialty knowledge related to their AFSCs. While completion of some of these courses is often required for enlisted personnel to advance in their careers, the courses have the added benefit of being a valuable source of college credit. The institute offers career development courses in the career fields listed below:

Course Title	Career Field Number
Aircrew Operations	(1A)
Command Control Systems Operations	(1C)
Intelligence	(1N)
Safety	(1S)
Aircrew Protection	(1T)
Weather	(1W)
Manned Aerospace Maintenance	(2A)
Communications-Electronics Systems	(2E)
Fuels	(2F)
Logistics Plans	(2G)
Missile and Space Systems Maintenance	(2M)
Precision Measurement	(2P)
Maintenance Management Systems	(2R)
Supply	(2S)
Transportation and Vehicle Maintenance	(2T)
Munitions and Weapons	(2W)
Information Management	(3A)
Communications-Computer Systems	(3C)
Civil Engineering	(3E)
Civil Engineering (Fire Protection)	(3E)
Morale, Welfare, Recreation, and Services	(3M)
Public Affairs	(3N)
Security Police	(3P)
Printing Management	(3R)
Mission Support	(3S)
Manpower	(3U)
Visual Information	(3V)
Medical (Except 4Y)	(4)
Dental	(4Y)
Paralegal	(5J)
Chaplain Service Support	(5R)
Contracting	(6C)
Financial	(6F)
Special Investigations	(7S)
Reporting Identifiers	(9S)

College Credit for AFIADL Career Development Courses

Over 500 AFIADL courses are recommended for college credit. The credit recommendations include credit in the upper and lower divisions of the baccalaureate and associate programs, along with recommendations for credit in vocational, technical, and certificate programs. While a complete list of these courses and recommendations is not possible in this book, a sample of some of the American Council on Education credit recommendations are included below. The codes are keyed to the Air Force career field members listed above. For a complete list of AFIADL courses and the corresponding credit recommendations, visit the AFIADL website at *www.maxwell.af.mil/au/afiadl/* or see your nearest Air Force Education Center.

06610 - Semester hours: 4 (2 Voc)
AF 1408-0091; completion date: August 1992 to present; 1 semester hour in applied mathematics (Voc); 1 semester hour in retailing (pricing) (Voc); 2 semester hours in business mathematics; 2 semester hours in purchasing: April 93

1A151C - Semester hours: 6
AF 1704-0294; completion date: August 1994 to present; 3 semester hours in aircraft and ground equipment systems inspection, 1 in basic aircraft systems, 1 in aircraft powerplants, and 1 in meteorology: June 1998

1C051 - Semester hours: 3
AF 1704-0297; completion date: December 1996 to present; 3 semester hours in basic airport operations (within a civil engineering or aeronautics curriculum): June 1998

1C052 - Semester hours: 2
AF 1406-0103; completion date: April 1996 to present; 2 semester hours in human resource management systems: June 1998

1C251A - Semester hours: 3
AF 1704-0296; completion date: October 1994 to present; 3 semester hours in air traffic control procedures: June 1998

1C251B - Semester hours: 2
AF 0801-0006; completion date: November 1995 to present; 1 semester hour in small-arms training, and 1 in first aid/hazardous material response: June 1998

1C551 - Semester hours: 2
AF 1715-0754; completion date: January 1990 to present; 2 semester hours in introduction to radar systems: June 1998

1T051 - Semester hours: 3
AF 1406-0105; completion date: October 1996 to present; in the lower-division baccalaureate/associate degree category, 1 semester hour in climate and environment, and 1 in human physiology and medical first aid: June 1998: in the upper-division baccalaureate category, 1 semester hour in instructional techniques and methods: June 1998

10213 - Semester hours: 3
AF 1722-0001; completion date: January 1997 to present; 3 semester hours in fire service management: November 98

10214 - Semester hours: 3
AF 1722-0002; completion date: July 1997 to present; 3 semester hours in principles of management: November 98

2A051 - Semester hour: 4
AF 1715-0849; completion date May 1994 to present; 3 semester hours in electronic systems troubleshooting and maintenance, and 1 in personnel supervision: June 1998

2A373A - Semester hours: 3
AF 1704-0324; completion date: February 1996 to present; 1 semester hour in personnel supervision, 1 in aircraft fuel systems, and 1 in aircraft hydraulic systems: June 1998

2A552B - Semester hours: 7
AF 1704-0320; completion date: October 1995 to present; 3 semester hours in turbine engine overhaul and inspection, 2 in airworthiness inspections, 1 in aircraft hydraulic systems, and 1 in aircraft assembly and rigging: June 1998

2A753 - Semester hours: 6
AF 1723-0017; completion date: December 1995 to present; 1 semester hour in aircraft cleaning and corrosion control, 1 in aircraft

drawings, 1 in aircraft fluid lines and fittings, 1 in aircraft composite, structural technician, and 2 in aircraft sheetmetal structures: June 1998

2E153B - Semester hours: 4
AF 1715-0829; completion date: January 1996 to present; 2 semester hours in introduction to computer theory or introduction to microprocessors, and 2 in introduction to communications theory: June 1998

23153 - Semester hours: 9
AF 0505-0005; completion date: January 1992 to present; 6 semester hours in introduction to radio-TV film, lower-division baccalaureate/associate; 3 semester hours in introduction to radio-TV film, upper-division baccalaureate: June 1994

3E052B - Semester hours: 6
AF 1714-0054; completion date: March 1997 to present; 2 semester hours in diesel engine systems; 2 semester hours in electrical power production engine maintenance; 2 semester hours in electrical power plant maintenance: November 98

3E151A - Semester hours: 2
AF 1701-0014; completion date: June 1998 to present; 2 semester hours in fundamentals of heating, ventilation, air conditioning/ refrigeration systems: November 98

3E351B - Semester hours: 3
AF 1723-0023; completion date: May 1997 to present; in the lower-division baccalaureate/associate degree category, 3 semester hours in residential sheet metal fabrication: November 98

3E351C - Semester hours: 3
AF 1710-0042; completion date: July 1997 to present; in the lower-division baccalaureate/associate degree category, 2 semester hours in residential carpentry, and 1 semester hour in concrete and masonry: November 98

3E451A - Semester hours: 3
AF 1710-0043; completion date: June 1998 to present; in the lower-division baccalaureate/associate degree category, 3 semester hours in residential and light commercial plumbing: November 98

4D051 - Semester hours: 8
AF 0104-0004; completion date: April 1996 to present; 1 semester hour in introduction to health profession careers; 2 semester hours in food service and production; 3 semester hours in diet therapy (clinical dietetics); 2 semester hours in food management; 1 semester hour in food personnel management: November 98

4P051B - Semester hours: 5
AF 0799-0011; completion date: July 1996 to present; in the lower-division baccalaureate/associate degree category, 3 semester hours in anatomy and physiology of body systems; 2 semester hours in body endocrine system: November 98

41152A - Semester Hours: 14
AF 1704-0264; completion date: April 1992 to present; 3 semester hours in internal combustion engine fundamentals; 3 semester hours in electrical fundamentals; 2 semester hours in industrial electricity; 3 semester hours in air conditioning principles; 3 semester hours in maintenance administration, lower-division baccalaureate/associate degree: April 93

54252B - Semester hours: 6
AF 1714-0040; completion date: August 1993 to present; 2 semester hours in diesel engine systems maintenance; 2 in electrical power plant maintenance; 2 in electrical power production engine maintenance, lower-division baccalaureate/associate: June 1994

70250 - Semester hours: 2
AF 1406-0045; completion date: August 1991 to present; 1 semester hour in records management; 1 semester hour in office administration: April 93

82170 - Semester hours: 5
AF 1728-0039; completion date: September 1981 to present; 3 semester hours in criminal investigation; 2 semester hours in interview and interrogation: September 86

89370 - Semester hours: 1
AF 1408-0112; completion date: February 1993 to present; 1 semester hour in supervisory management, lower-division baccalaureate/associate: June 1994

91150 - Semester hours: 1
AF 0709-0032; completion date: February 1982 to present; 1 semester hour in first aid, lower-division baccalaureate/associate degree: May 88

91255 - Semester hours: 5
AF 0706-0003; completion date: February 1983 to present; 5 semester hours in optometric technology, lower-division baccalaureate/associate degree: May 88

More Information about AFIADL
To obtain more information about AFIADL, you can visit the AFIADL website at *www.maxwell.af.mil/au/afiadl/*. If you prefer, you can call AFIADL at (334) 953-4620 or write to Air Force Institute for Advanced Distributed Learning, 50 South Turner Boulevard, Maxwell AFB-Gunter Annex, AL 36118.

PART V

NONTRADITIONAL EDUCATION RESOURCES: PROGRAMS FOR ALL

10

More on College Credit for Military Experience

Each branch of the armed forces provides different ways for servicemembers to obtain college credit for their military experiences. As shown in chapters 3, 5, and 8, the Army has the Army/American Council on Education Registry Transcript System; the Navy and Marine Corps have the Sailor/Marine American Council on Education Registry Transcript; and the Air Force has the Community College of the Air Force. Servicemembers, regardless of service, also may use either DD Form 295, *Application for Evaluation of Learning Experiences during Military Service*, or DD Form 2586, *Verification of Military Experience and Training*.

DD FORM 295

DD Form 295 is officially known as the *Application for Evaluation of Learning Experiences during Military Service*. DD Form 295 was used extensively by servicemembers to receive credit for their military experiences and training before AARTS or SMART was implemented. Due to the fact that not all servicemembers are eligible to use AARTS or SMART, DD Form 295 remains in service.

How Do You Use It?

The form is available at most military education centers or from your local military personnel officer. You should complete the form with the assistance of your education officer, taking great care to ensure that all data are entered correctly. Complete columns 1 through 15. The data you provide, such as rank, address, and courses completed, are essentially the same information as that found on the AARTS or SMART. Your education officer or personnel official should complete all information required in sections 16 through 18. Do not use abbreviations to describe your official training or courses,

**APPLICATION FOR THE EVALUATION OF
LEARNING EXPERIENCES DURING MILITARY SERVICE**

_____
(Date) (YYYYMMDD)

TO: *(Name and address of educational institution,
agency, or employer)*

EVALUATION REQUEST FOR:

_____
(Name of Applicant)

_____
(Social Security Number)

ATTENTION:

Dear Official:

The applicant named above has requested that the attached summary of educational achievements, accomplished while in the Armed Forces of the United States, be forwarded to you for review and evaluation.

The American Council on Education publishes the *Guide to the Evaluation of Educational Experiences in the Armed Services.* The Guide series contains postsecondary credit recommendations for selected military courses and occupations. The 1954-1989 Guide contains recommendations spanning the dates 1/1954 - 12/1989, and should be kept as a permanent resource. The current edition contains credit recommendations from 1/1990 to the present, and is published every two years. In addition, supplemental handbooks are issued at 6-month intervals between Guide publications. The handbook contains recommendations for all evaluations conducted after the publication of the current Guide.

This form contains a record of a Service member's military courses and occupations. It should be signed by a military official whose signature certifies that the information that is entered on the form is accurate and is taken directly from original records. ACE ID numbers are entered in column 18 by military education officers.

The American Council on Education maintains an advisory service to provide credit recommendations for courses, tests, and occupations that cannot be located in any of the Guide publications. If ACE ID numbers have been entered into column 18, it is not necessary to submit this form to ACE. If there are questions about any of the entries, the institutional official may contact ACE for additional information. Credit recommendations are not provided to institutions at the applicant's request.

Authorized persons may submit questions to ACE at the following address: American Council on Education, Center for Adult Learning and Educational Credentials, One Dupont Circle, Washington, DC 20036-1193, ATTN: Military Evaluations. Telephone: (202) 939-9470; Fax: (202) 775-8578; e-mail: mileval@ace.nche.edu.

The evaluation of this applicant's learning experiences, as well as any guidance you may provide, should be sent directly to the applicant at the address shown in Block 6 on page 3.

Sincerely,

_____
(Education Officer)

DD FORM 295, APR 2000   PREVIOUS EDITION IS OBSOLETE.   Page 1 of 4 Pages

PRIVACY ACT STATEMENT

AUTHORITY: 10 U.S.C. 2007; P.L. 104-106; and E.O. 9397.

PRINCIPAL PURPOSE(S): To facilitate an individual's request for evaluation of educational experiences while in the military services.

ROUTINE USE(S): None.

DISCLOSURE: Voluntary; however, you will not be evaluated for your educational experiences during military service if you fail to provide requested information.

INSTRUCTIONS TO APPLICANT

DD Form 295 is for your convenience in applying for evaluation of your educational experiences during military service. Give as much detailed information as possible. Include additional information on separate sheets, if necessary. Do not use abbreviations.

You are encouraged to write a preliminary letter to the school or agency concerned, explaining your interest in its evaluation of your records for the continuance of your education. Training, correspondence study, or special experiences not described on this form, which you believe would be of interest to those reviewing your case, should be included in this letter.

The applicant should:

a. Complete items 1 through 14.

b. If you have attended college or completed any college correspondence courses, ask that college to send a transcript to the Registrar of the evaluating agency that this form is addressed to. DO NOT LIST ANY COLLEGE OR UNIVERSITY COURSES ON THIS FORM.

c. If you have completed any college-level standardized examinations for credit, such as USAFI or DANTES Subject Standardized Tests, or CLEP, ask the appropriate agency to send a score report to the Registrar of the evaluating agency that this form is addressed to. DO NOT LIST ANY EXAMINATIONS ON THIS FORM.

d. After completion, submit this DD Form 295 to the Certifying Officer.

INSTRUCTIONS TO CERTIFYING OFFICER
(Custodian of Personnel Records)

DD Form 295 is intended to provide factual information that schools and other evaluating agencies require for evaluation of the applicant's educational achievement. By your signature, you verify that all information is accurate and taken directly from military records. CERTIFYING OFFICERS WILL NOT MAKE RECOMMENDATIONS REGARDING CREDIT TO BE AWARDED.

The certifying officer should:

a. Complete items 15 through 17, in ink (or type). Supplemental sheets may be used.

b. Insure that the information provided in Section II is documented in the applicant's Service Record. Names of schools or courses should not be abbreviated.

c. Send this DD Form 295 to the Education Officer.

INSTRUCTIONS TO EDUCATION OFFICER

The education officer should:

a. Complete item 18.

b. Counsel the service member.

c. Complete page 1. The name and address of the evaluating agency should be the same as that listed at the top of page 3 of this form.

PAGE 1 IS IN ADDITION TO, AND NOT A SUBSTITUTE FOR, THE LETTER TO BE WRITTEN TO THE EVALUATING AGENCY BY THE APPLICANT.

d. Mail DD Form 295 directly to the designated evaluating agency.

DD FORM 295, APR 2000

**APPLICATION FOR THE EVALUATION OF LEARNING EXPERIENCES
DURING MILITARY SERVICE**

TO *(Name and address of educational institution, agency, or employer)*

SECTION I - TO BE COMPLETED BY APPLICANT

1. NAME *(Last, First, Middle Initial)*	2. GRADE/RANK OR RATING	3. SOCIAL SECURITY NO.	4. PREVIOUS SERVICE NUMBER(S)

5. PRESENT BRANCH OF SERVICE *(Includes National Guard and Reserve components)*

ARMY	NAVY	AIR FORCE	MARINE CORPS	COAST GUARD

6. APPLICANT'S MAILING ADDRESS FOR REPLY FROM EDUCATIONAL INSTITUTION

7. DATE OF BIRTH *(YYYYMMDD)*	8. PERMANENT HOME ADDRESS

CIVILIAN EDUCATION

9. HIGHEST GRADE OF SCHOOL COMPLETED *(X one)*

6	7	8	9	10	11	12

10. HIGHEST YEAR OF COLLEGE COMPLETED *(X one)* | 11. COLLEGE DEGREE EARNED *(X if applicable)*

NONE	FRESHMAN *(1 - 29 S.H.)*	SOPHOMORE *(33 - 59 S.H.)*	JUNIOR *(60 - 89 S.H.)*	SENIOR *(90 - 100 S.H.)*	ASSOCIATE	BACHELOR

12. EDUCATIONAL INSTITUTION LAST ATTENDED

a. NAME	b. MAILING ADDRESS

13. MILITARY CORRESPONDENCE COURSES COMPLETED *(The applicant should attach a copy of the course completion letter or certificate.)*

	a. COURSE NAME *(If no courses were taken, print NONE)*	b. ACE GUIDE COURSE OR OCCUPATION IDENTIFICATION NUMBER	c. COURSE SPONSOR *(AIPD, MCI, ECI, CGI)*	d. DATE COURSE COMPLETED *(YYYYMMDD)*
(1)				
(2)				
(3)				
(4)				
(5)				
(6)				
(7)				
(8)				
(9)				
(10)				
(11)				
(12)				
(13)				
(14)				
(15)				
(16)				
(17)				
(18)				
(19)				
(20)				

14. APPLICANT CERTIFICATION: I have read the Privacy Act Statement on Page 2.

a. SIGNATURE	b. DATE SIGNED *(YYYYMMDD)*

DD FORM 295, APR 2000

SECTION II - TO BE COMPLETED BY CERTIFYING OFFICER
(Read Instructions on Page 2 before completing this page)

15. FORMAL SERVICE SCHOOLS ATTENDED *(If 40 hours in 5 consecutive days, or if longer than 32 hours in 5 consecutive days.) (If none, print NONE.)*

a. COURSE TITLE *(Do Not Abbreviate)*	b. MILITARY COURSE NUMBER	c. NAME OF SCHOOL, CITY, STATE	d. DATE ENTERED *(YYYYMMDD)*	e. LENGTH *(In weeks)* *(Note 1)*	f. DATE COMPLETED *(YYYYMMDD)*	g. FINAL MARK AND/OR CLASS STANDING *(Note 2)*	18. ACE GUIDE COURSE OR OCCUPATION IDENTIFICATION NO. *(To be filled out in Education Center)*
(1)							
(2)							
(3)							
(4)							
(5)							
(6)							

16. MILITARY OCCUPATIONAL HISTORY

a. MILITARY SPEC. CODE *(MOS, AFSC, Rate, etc.)* *(Note 3)*	b. MILITARY OCCUPATIONAL TITLE *(Do Not Abbreviate)*	c. DATES HELD (1) FROM *(YYYYMMDD)*	c. DATES HELD (2) TO *(YYYYMMDD)*	d. MOS/SQT/SDT SCORE *(For Army Enlisted Personnel)* *(Note 4)*
(1)				
(2)				
(3)				

NOTES:
1. Print **SP** if course length was self paced.
2. If information is available, give grade received. If class standing is shown, give number in class, e.g., 10 in 241.
3. List most recent skill levels or grade.
4. MOS/SQT/SDT Evaluation Score and date of evaluation.

THIS APPLICATION MUST BE SIGNED BY AN OFFICER OR A DULY AUTHORIZED NONCOMMISSIONED OFFICER.
I certify that the information contained herein has been compared with official records, and that this information is correct.

17. CERTIFYING OFFICER

a. NAME *(Print or Type)*	b. GRADE/RANK	c. MILITARY ADDRESS *(Include ZIP Code)*
d. SIGNATURE	e. DATE SIGNED *(YYYYMMDD)*	

DD FORM 295, APR 2000

Page 4 of 4 Pages

because certifying officials may not know the meaning of unfamiliar acronyms or abbreviations. After you complete the form, sign it and take it to your certifying officer, usually a personnel official. The certifying official verifies the accuracy of the data entered on DD Form 295 using your personnel records. If your personnel records are inaccurate, your DD Form 295 will likely be inaccurate or the certifying official will refuse to certify it. After the form is complete and verified, take it to your education officer for research and counseling. The education officer will complete column 19 using the *ACE Guide/Handbook to the Evaluation of Educational Experiences in the Armed Services*. If the education officer cannot locate the correct exhibit, section 19 is left blank. All identifiers (title, number, location, dates, and length) must match those in the *ACE Guide*. The education officer then completes page 1 of the form, signs it, and mails it to the college from which the servicemember is requesting credit. DD Form 295 should not be sent to the American Council on Education (ACE) unless the courses are not found in the *ACE Guide*. It is recommended that the servicemember provide the college with a cover letter requesting it to review DD Form 295. Most college officials will usually grant credit to the servicemember as long as it is appropriate and justifiable. It is a good idea to suggest that DD Form 295 be forwarded to ACE if the school has any questions.

DD FORM 2586

DD Form 2586, better known as the VMET (*Verification of Military Experience and Training*) document is an overview of a servicemember's military career. The VMET database contains information on active-duty, reserve, and National Guard members who have served on or after 1 October 1990.

The VMET document verifies a servicemember's military experience and training and translates them into civilian terms. While the primary purpose of the VMET is to help you create a resume and complete job applications, it also can be used to support the awarding of training or academic credit. For some skills, the VMET can provide certification to allow waiver of apprenticeship and testing requirements.

Data Listed on the VMET Document

The VMET document includes reported military experience history from September 1975 to the present with supporting descriptive data and all available military training history (course completions only) with supporting descriptive data. Also included on the document is related civilian occupation data, language proficiency data, and off-duty education (USMC only).

The military occupation and training codes listed on the document are reported by the four military services. The supporting descriptive data come from the four military services' occupational/training sources and the American Council on Education (ACE). The occupation descriptions are standard for the occupation and therefore are not necessarily the duties you performed while holding the occupation. The VMET is divided into the following sections:

Heading: the heading on the first page of the form lists demographic data such as name, date of birth, social security number, and years of service. Also, a date of information is listed on the form that indicates the as-of date of an individual's work experience data.

Work experience: work experience data (occupation codes) are listed in "occupation clusters" in reverse chronological order (most recent to oldest) following the heading. Clusters are created for each unique occupation for each service and military pay category (enlisted, officer, and warrant). The clusters assimilate all data over time relating to the occupation code. The cluster begins with the occupation code and title, followed by "held data" for the code. The "held data" include pay grade/skill level or rank/rating and the dates that occupation was held. Descriptions for the occupations are listed next, followed by academic course credit recommendations when available. The last segment of the cluster contains related civilian occupations (title and code) when available.

Additional qualifications (AQs): additional qualification data (when available) are listed next, following the last work experience cluster.

Training history: military training course completions are listed next in reverse chronological order. Data for the same course code are "date clustered" when the course was taken more than once during a person's career. The course listings contain available information for title, location, duration, description, and academic course credit recommendation.

Off-duty education: off-duty education is provided when it is available for members with current or previous military service in the Marine Corps. This information is not available from the other services.

Languages: language proficiency data are listed last when available.

Obtaining a Copy of Your VMET Document

The VMET document is free. Servicemembers and former servicemembers can obtain a copy of theirs from VMET's website: *www.dmdc.-*

osd.mil/vmet. The VMET, as delivered via the web, is considered an official document.

Most military installations have a transition assistance support office through which you can also obtain your VMET document. To locate the facility nearest to you, consult your local base directory for the following type of offices:

Army: Army Career and Alumni Program (ACAP) Center. If there is no listing for an ACAP center, contact the Army Community Services (ACS) Office.

Navy: Transition Assistance Management Program (TAMP), Family Service Center, Mobile Job Assistance Team, or the command career counselor.

Air Force: active-duty members should contact the Family Support Center or Military Personnel Flight; reserve and Air National Guard members should contact their servicing military personnel office; separated and retired members should contact HQ AFPC/DPPTT (transition and relocation operations) at DSN 665-2631 or (800) 581-9437.

Marine Corps: Career Resource Management Center or Family Service Center.

Information Included on the VMET Document

Military service on or after 1 October 1990, along with any contiguous work experience as far back as September 1975, is displayed on your VMET document regardless of service or component. All available training data, regardless of service or component, is also listed on the VMET.

As for ACE credit, ACE has not evaluated any of the occupations for the Air Force, any of the commissioned officer occupations for the Army and Navy (except LDO and NWO (designator) for the Navy), and most Marine Corps occupations. Course evaluations conducted by ACE do not include all courses offered by the armed services.

Information Not Listed on the VMET Document

Although the VMET document provides verification of experience and training as of a certain date, it does not display all of the data found in a member's official military records. For example, data for many additional duties and efficiency/performance report data are not available, so they cannot be listed on DD Form 2586. Therefore, the VMET is not a stand-alone document; it should be supplemented with information on your performance reports, training certificates, transcripts, diplomas, and other documentation. All these tools taken together provide a more complete picture of your military career and achievements.

The VMET database does not contain experience history prior to September 1975. Additionally, before January 1993 data was not captured and summarized on a monthly basis; therefore, the dates of your experience may not be correct. Electronically stored data is the primary source of data for the VMET. The services began storing data electronically at different times, and this accounts for the differences in data availability. Training history data are limited prior to fiscal year 1984 for the Army, fiscal year 1978 for the Navy, fiscal year 1970 for the Air Force, and fiscal year 1967 for the Marine Corps.

VMET Variations from Service to Service

Army
The VMET documents of Army commissioned officers do not display any work experience data. For these officers, a paragraph on the document provides a reference for obtaining work experience information. Experience clusters are created for each unique warrant and enlisted occupation code and for each unique officer occupation code in the cases where the individual's latest VMET work experience was not as an Army officer. Clusters can include primary and duty occupation information, followed by a separate section for additional qualifications (AQs), when applicable. Examples of AQs listed are secondary occupations, additional skills identifier (ASI), special qualifications identifier (SQI), and skills identifier (SI).

Navy
Navy work experience clusters are created for each unique enlisted, warrant, and officer occupation code held, and they include primary and duty occupations held. For officer and warrant officer, the primary and duty occupations are displayed as Navy designator and Navy officer billet classification (NOBC), respectively. Experience clusters are followed by additional qualifications (AQs), when applicable. Examples of AQs listed are Navy enlisted classification (NEC), additional qualification designation (AQD), and subspecialty (SSP).

Air Force
Air Force work experience includes primary and duty Air Force specialty codes (AFSCs) held, including special duty identifier (SDI), reporting identifier (RI), chief enlisted manager (CEM), and officer command/director

AFSCs. Experience clusters are created for each unique AFSC using the set of all non-skill-level AFSC digits for the AFSC. Therefore SDI, RI, CEM, command/director AFSCs, and some enlisted skill-level 9 AFSCs (depending on what 7 level AFSC the individual held) are uniquely clustered, whereas clusters for all other AFSCs held contain all skill levels held for the AFSC. Experience clusters are followed by a separate section for additional qualifications (AQs), when applicable. Authorized prefixes are the only Air Force AQ type listed in the AQ section.

Marine Corps
Marine Corps work experience clusters are created for each unique enlisted, warrant, or officer occupation code. The clusters can contain primary, duty, and/or secondary occupations held. Secondary occupations can be additional qualifications (AQs), but they are listed within occupation clusters, rather than separately in an AQ section. When available, VMET documents contain information on off-duty education.

VMET Document Eligibility
All Army, Navy, Marine Corps, and Air Force servicemembers with active, reserve, or National Guard service on or after 1 October 1990 are eligible to receive the VMET document. Ideally, active-duty servicemembers should receive the VMET at least 120 days before their separation date. Since January 2001, all servicemembers, including reservists and National Guard personnel, have been able to receive the document via the VMET website: *www.dmdc.osd.mil/vmet.*

Making Corrections to the VMET Document
The VMET system is fully reliant on information submitted by the services for demographic, occupation, and training data. Errors listed on the document are usually the result of erroneous data submitted by the services or errors in service occupation/course descriptions. Also, errors may occur in the process of handling/interpreting the data.

To correct errors, you must contact your parent service. When a correction is possible, but would not result in any new descriptive data not already contained on the form, then the services usually do not make the change. Also, in some cases, errors cannot be corrected after a member's separation or retirement. There is no simple process to make changes to an individual member's DD Form 2586. The changes must pass through official channels and can take months. To make corrections, follow the procedures identified for the specific military service, as indicated below.

Army

Soldiers that identify an error or omission of data on their VMET document should call the Army VMET help line at (800) 258-8638 or send an e-mail to *ArmyVmet@hoffman.army.mil*.

Navy

All U.S. Navy individuals should discuss report errors with their command career counselor and/or personnel officer. A review of local records with data on file via microfiche records may be required. If corrections to the master personnel file are warranted, your personnel officer should initiate corrective action with assistance from Naval Personnel Command (PERS-313.)

General document information is available from the Transition Assistance Management Program, Navy Personnel Command, Personnel and Family Readiness Branch (PERS-662C), 5720 Integrity Drive, Millington, TN 38055-6620; DSN: 882-4384 or (901) 874-4384; e-mail: *p662c12a@persnet.navy.mil*. The Transition Assistance Management Program staff cannot make any changes to your VMET document.

Air Force

If a member desires to discuss what he or she believes is an omission or error, he or she may contact HQ AFPC/DPPTT (transition and relocation operations) at DSN 665-2631 or (800) 581-9437 or e-mail *VMET@afpc.randolph.af.mil*. In order for the Air Force to provide the best possible service, members contacting AFPC/DPPTT must include their social security number.

Marine Corps

All active-duty and reserve marines shall report to their local administration office with official documentation verifying corrected information for their SRB/OQR and the MCTFS database for entry by the unit diary clerk. They can also contact the Mobility and Mobilization Support Branch at Headquarters, U.S. Marine Corps (HQMC), Manpower and Reserve Affairs (M&RA), Personal and Family Readiness Division (MR), Transition Assistance Management Program (MRM), 3280 Russell Road, Marsh Center, 4th Floor, Quantico, VA 22134-5103. The phone number is (703) 784-9523 or DSN 278-9523, and the fax number is (703) 784-9825.

11

College Credit
by Examination

Examinations for college credit are nationally and internationally recognized testing programs that have been evaluated and approved by the American Council on Education (ACE) to grant college credit for experience, knowledge, and training obtained outside the traditional classroom setting. These examinations, which are listed on the following pages, represent the single greatest nontraditional source of recognized college credit. Among the examinations covered are those of Excelsior College Examinations (ECE) (formerly known as the Regents College Examinations, or RCE), the Institute for Certification of Computing Professionals (ICCP), the College Level Examination Program (CLEP), and the Defense Activity for Non-Traditional Education Support (DANTES). These testing methods are the best known and most widely used testing programs for gaining college credit through nontraditional methods. Other testing systems include the Graduate Record Examinations (GRE), Thomas Edison College Examination Program (TECEP), the Ohio University Testing course credit by examination (CCE), advanced placement (AP) examinations, and New York University (NYU) foreign language proficiency tests. Except for the GRE exams, these testing systems are not widely available to all servicemembers and are not detailed in this book. Additional information on these systems can usually be obtained at the military education center.

HOW ARE THESE TESTS DEVELOPED?
The major goal of these examinations is to measure learning in a subject area, regardless of the method used, against the same standard of learning gained from a college classroom. A standard practice in developing these tests is to administer them to a sample of college and university students who are completing equivalent courses. This way, the achievement levels on

the tests can be compared directly with the achievement of college students who have completed the course for which credit is intended. This process of nationally norming the examinations ensures their validity and reliability and provides data for determining the passing score of each test.

TAKING THE EXAMINATIONS

All examinations for college credit detailed in this chapter are free to active-duty military personnel. Furthermore, none of the testing programs addressed on the following pages has any prerequisites. Keep in mind, however, that these tests are designed to measure knowledge that you gained outside the traditional classroom. It is unlikely that you could get lucky and pass a test with no prior learning of the subject. Some education centers, in an attempt to keep servicemembers from trying to get lucky and pass a test, now require them to take a pretest. If a servicemember does not score high enough on the pretest to justify taking the real test, the education officer often recommends a study plan. It may be necessary to register for these examinations several days in advance at some education centers.

All the examinations listed can be taken at your military education center. To find the center nearest to you, consult appendix C in this book. It provides a complete list of all known permanent military education centers throughout the world.

COLLEGE CREDIT FOR THE TESTS

Each examination offered through ECE, CLEP, and DANTES is listed on the following pages, along with the ACE college credit recommendations for that test. These examinations cover a wide variety of topics, and their content is based on material covered in equivalent college courses. Tests can be taken to earn college credit in courses ranging from statistics to the fundamentals of electronics to the Civil War and Reconstruction to microbiology. The tests themselves, however, do not award college credit; a student must have his or her official test results forwarded to the school from which college credit is being sought. That school then evaluates the test results and awards the appropriate credit based on the ACE recommendations and its own policies.

Schools Awarding Credit for These Examinations

Two of the schools detailed in this book, Excelsior College and Thomas Edison State College, accept all ACE recommendations for awarding college credit. All other schools listed in this book accept most ACE recommendations for awarding college credit for examinations. To determine the acceptability of a specific testing program at a particular school, servicemembers should visit their education officer and ask to see the *Servicemembers Opportunity Colleges Guide*. This guide has over 1,000 pages of schools that work closely with military personnel, and it details which testing programs are accepted at each of these institutions. Servicemember Opportunity Colleges (SOC) are covered in chapter 15. Most schools also publish the acceptability of college credit examinations in their catalogs.

Grades Assigned for These Examinations

Examinations for college credit are assigned a numerical score. Some schools will convert this numerical score to a letter grade. Most schools, however, annotate a passing numerical score with a "P" on the college transcripts. For those examinations in which a passing score was not obtained, most schools simply will make no annotation on the transcript. In other words, if one passes the examination, then it is placed on the college transcript; if one fails, it is not. Those institutions that do convert passing numerical scores to traditional letter grades maintain their own conversion scales. You should contact your institution to determine whether it uses a conversion system and, if so, the specific grade ranges.

Difference between Lower- and Upper-Division Baccalaureate Credit

All college credit applied toward a four-year bachelor degree is classified as either lower- or upper-division credit. Lower-division credit is awarded for general knowledge or courses normally taken during the first or second year of college. Most introductory and intermediate courses and knowledge, or courses taken at a community college or two-year college, are recognized for lower-division credit. Lower-division courses normally begin with the number 1 or 2. For example, freshman English Composition may be numbered ENG 101 or ENG 1015.

Upper-division credit is awarded for advanced knowledge or courses normally taken during the third and fourth years of college. Such courses and knowledge are normally more intensive than lower-division courses and often have prerequisites. Upper-division courses normally begin with the number 3 or 4. For example, a senior-level history course such as Special Research Topics in History may be numbered HIS 460 or HIS 4521.

EXCELSIOR COLLEGE EXAMINATIONS

There are forty college-level examinations in the ECE series. Approximately 900 colleges and universities grant college credit based on ECE exams. Unlike other examinations, the ECE exams are automatically converted and reported as letter grades. In order to receive credit for an ECE exam, an individual must score a C or higher on it. Although most of these examinations are multiple-choice tests, some are essay tests. These examinations are offered in the arts and sciences, business, education, and nursing and are listed below.

Test Title	Recommended Credit (SH)
Arts and Sciences	
Abnormal Psychology	3 (U)
American Dream (E)	6 (U)
Anatomy and Physiology	6 (L)
English Composition (E)	6 (L)
Ethics: Theory and Practice	3 (U)
Foundations of Gerontology	3 (U)
History of Nazi Germany (E)	3 (U)
Life Span Developmental Psychology	3 (L)
Microbiology	3 (U)
Pathophysiology	3 (U)
Psychology of Adulthood and Aging	3 (U)
Religions of the World (E)	3 (U)
Research Methods in Psychology	3 (U)
Statistics	3 (L)
World Population	3 (U)
Business	
Business Policy and Strategy (E)	3 (U)
Human Resource Management	3 (U)
Labor Relations	3 (U)
Organizational Behavior	3 (U)
Production/Operations Management	3 (L)
Education	
Reading Instruction in the Elementary School	6 (U)
Nursing (Associate)	
Occupational Strategies in Nursing	3 (L)
Nursing Concepts 1	4 (L)
Nursing Concepts 2	4 (L)
Nursing Concepts 3	4 (L)

Test Title	Recommended Credit (SH)
Differences in Nursing Care: Area A (modified)	4 (L)
Differences in Nursing Care: Area B	5 (L)
Differences in Nursing Care: Area C	5 (L)
Fundamentals of Nursing	8 (L)
Maternal and Child Nursing	6 (L)
Maternity Nursing	3 (L)
Nursing (baccalaureate)	
Adult Nursing	8 (U)
Health Restoration: Area I	4 (U)
Health Restoration: Area II	4 (U)
Health Support A: Health Promotion and Health Protection	4 (U)
Health Support B: Community Health Nursing	4 (U)
Maternal and Child Nursing	8 (U)
Professional Strategies in Nursing	4 (U)
Psychiatric/Mental Health Nursing	8 (U)
Research in Nursing	3 (U)

Abbreviations: E, essay examination; SH, semester hours of college credit; L, recommended for lower-division baccalaureate credit; U, recommended for upper-division baccalaureate credit.

ECE Essay Tests
The following are brief descriptions of the type of knowledge tested in each of the ECE essay examinations. This information can be used as guide when studying.

American Dream
This test reflects an interdisciplinary course of study that examines both the conflict and the consensus that resulted as groups and individuals struggled to define and shape the American dream prior to the Civil War. It draws from U.S. literature, history, and political science.

English Composition
This test is based on the knowledge normally obtained from an introductory, two-semester course in English composition. It measures the ability to write an effective proposal, to analyze and respond appropriately to written arguments, and to recognize the strengths and weaknesses of a piece of writing.

History of Nazi Germany

This test reflects a study of the history of post-World War I Germany through World War II. It includes the rise of the National Socialists to power, aspects of life in Nazi Germany, foreign policy, and war and society from 1939 to 1945.

Religions of the World

This test reflects an interdisciplinary course of study of the major religions as viewed in their social and historical contexts. This test requires a general knowledge of the concepts drawn from sociology, psychology, and philosophy. The individual should be able to analyze and compare the various religious beliefs and practices.

Business Policy and Strategy

This test corresponds to a one-semester, upper-division course in business policy and strategy. It requires the integration of facts and concepts from core business subjects, the application of these concepts to address business problems, and an understanding of the influence of business environments on solving business problems.

Preparation for ECE Multiple-Choice Tests

All of the ECE exams have corresponding informational study guides that provide an overview of each test. Depending on supply, your local military education center may provide these materials. Otherwise, servicemembers can download copies of the free study guides at *www.excelsior.edu* or call Excelsior College at (518) 464-8500 and request them. The study guides also contain information about the optional purchase or rental of audio- and videotapes and books designed to assist with test preparation.

INSTITUTE FOR CERTIFICATION OF COMPUTING PROFESSIONALS (ICCP) EXAMINATIONS

Excelsior College also offers sixteen different ICCP examinations, which the college uses to award college credit for professional knowledge in the field of computer science. The passing grade for all ICCP exams is 70 percent, the same grade required to use the exam toward ICCP certification requirements. These examinations cover subjects related to the computer sciences and are listed below along with the semester hour (SH) credits:

Test Title	Excelsior Credit (SH)
Business Information Systems	3 (L)
COBOL	3 (L)
BASIC	3 (L)
C Language	3 (L)
Communications	3 (U)
Core	3 (L)
C++ Language	3 (L)
Data Resource Management	3 (U)
Microcomputing and Networks	4 (L)
Management	3 (L)
PASCAL	3 (L)
Procedural Programming	3 (L)
Software Engineering	3 (U)
Systems Programming	3 (U/L)
Systems Security	3 (L)
Systems Development	3 (U)

Abbreviations: SH, semester hours of college credit; L, recommended for lower-division baccalaureate credit; U, recommended for upper-division baccalaureate credit.

Preparation for ICCP Tests
All of the ICCP examinations have corresponding exam content outlines that provide an overview of each test. Servicemembers can download copies of the content outlines from the ICCP website: *www.iccp.org*.

COLLEGE LEVEL EXAMINATION PROGRAM
There are two types of CLEP tests: CLEP general examinations and CLEP subject examinations.

CLEP general examinations measure college-level achievement in five basic areas of liberal arts: English composition, humanities, mathematics, natural sciences, and social sciences and history. The test questions on the general examinations relate to material usually presented in the first two years of a college curriculum. To pass any general examination, you must score 420 or higher. These examinations are as follows:

CLEP GENERAL EXAMINATIONS

Test Title	Recommended Credit (SH)
English Composition (without essay)	6 (L)
Social Sciences and History	6 (L)
Natural Sciences	6 (L)
Humanities	6 (L)
Mathematics	6 (L)
English Composition (with essay)	6 (L)

Abbreviations: SH, semester hours of college credit; L, recommended for lower-division baccalaureate credit.

CLEP subject examinations measure college-level learning for specific college courses. These tests measure knowledge of basic concepts, principles, relationships, and applications involved in college courses with similar titles. These tests are as follows:

CLEP SUBJECT EXAMINATIONS

Test Title	Recommended Credit (SH)	Minimum Score Required
Business		
Information Systems	3 (L)	52
Principles of Management	3 (L)	46
Principles of Accounting	6 (L)	45
Introductory Business Law	3 (L)	51
Principles of Marketing	3 (L)	50
Composition and Literature		
American Literature (E)	6 (L)	46
Analyzing and Interpreting Literature (E)	6 (L)	47
Composition, Freshman (E)	6 (L)	44
English Literature (E)	6 (L)	46

Test Title	Recommended Credit (SH)	Minimum Score Required
Foreign Languages		
French, level 1	6 (L)	39
French, level 2	12 (L)	45
German, level 1	6 (L)	36
German, level 2	12 (L)	42
Spanish, level 1	6 (L)	45
Spanish, level 2	12 (L)	50
History and Social Sciences		
American Government	3 (L)	47
United States History I: thru 1877	3 (L)	47
United States History II: 1865 to Present	3 (L)	46
Human Growth & Development	3 (L)	45
Introduction to Educational Psychology	3 (L)	47
Macroeconomics	3 (L)	44
Microeconomics	3 (L)	41
Introductory Psychology	3 (L)	47
Introductory Sociology	3 (L)	47
Western Civilization I: thru 1648	3 (L)	46
Western Civilization II: 1648 to Present	3 (L)	47
Science and Mathematics		
Calculus with elementary functions	6 (L)	41
Algebra	3 (L)	46
Trigonometry	3 (L)	50
Algebra-Trigonometry	3 (L)	45
General Biology	6 (L)	46
General Chemistry	6 (L)	50

Abbreviations: E, optional essay section available; SH, semester hours of college credit; L, recommended for lower-division baccalaureate credit.

Preparation for CLEP Examinations

Just like ECE exams, all CLEP exams have corresponding free informational study guides that provide an overview of each test. Most military education centers normally have a large supply of these pamphlets. If the materials are unavailable at the military education center, they can be requested by mail or phone at CLEP, P.O. Box 6600, Princeton, NJ 08541-6600; telephone: (609) 771-7865. *The Official Study Guide for the CLEP Examinations* can be ordered by calling (800) 323-7155. Additional information and materials may be available for downloading or for purchase via the CLEP website: *www.collegeboard.com/clep.*

DEFENSE ACTIVITY FOR NON-TRADITIONAL EDUCATION SUPPORT (DANTES)

The DANTES Subject Standardized Test (DSST) program is an extensive series of examinations in college and technical subjects. These tests are comparable to the final examinations in the equivalent college courses. These examinations are as follows:

Test Title	Recommended Credit (SH)	Minimum Score Required
Mathematics		
Fundamentals of College Algebra	3 (L)	47
Principles of Statistics	3 (L)	48
Social Science		
Art of the Western World	3 (L)	48
Contemporary Western Europe: 1946–1990	3 (L)	48
An Introduction to the Modern Middle East	3 (L)	44
Human/Cultural Geography	3 (L)	48
Rise and Fall of the Soviet Union	3 (U)	45
A History of the Vietnam War	3 (L)	49
The Civil War and Reconstruction	3 (U)	47
Foundations of Education	3 (L)	46
Life Span Developmental Psychology	3 (L)	46
General Anthropology	3 (L)	47
Drug and Alcohol Abuse	3 (U)	49
Introduction to Law Enforcement	3 (L)	45
Criminal Justice	3 (L)	49
Fundamentals of Counseling	3 (L)	45
Business		
Principles of Finance	3 (U)	46
Principles of Financial Accounting	3 (L)	49

Test Title	Recommended Credit (SH)	Minimum Score Required
Human Resource Management	3 (L)	48
Organizational Behavior	3 (L)	48
Principles of Supervision	3 (L)	46
Business Law II	3 (U)	52
Introduction to Computing	3 (L)	47
Introduction to Business	3 (L)	46
Money and Banking	3 (U)	48
Personal Finance	3 (L)	46
Management Information Systems	3 (U)	46
Business Mathematics	3 (L)	48
Physical Science		
Astronomy	3 (L)	48
Here's to Your Health	3 (L)	48
Environment and Humanity	3 (L)	46
Principles of Physical Science I	3 (L)	47
Physical Geology	3 (L)	46
Applied Technology		
Technical Writing	3 (L)	46
Humanities		
Ethics in America	3 (L)	46
Introduction to World Religions	3 (L)	49
Principles of Public Speaking	3 (L)	47

Abbreviations: E, optional essay section available; SH, semester hours of college credit; L, recommended for lower-division baccalaureate credit; U, recommended for upper-division baccalaureate credit.

Preparation for DANTES Tests
As with the ECE and CLEP exams, DANTES examinations have corresponding free informational study guides that can be obtained through the military education center. Materials can be downloaded by computer at *www.getcollegecredit.com* or requested by mail or phone at DANTES Program Office, Educational Testing Service, Rosedale Road, Princeton, NJ 08541; telephone: (609) 921-9000. An extensive DSST test preparation guide can be purchased by calling DSST customer service at (877) 471-9860.

Another excellent tool that can assist in preparing for examinations is the Annenberg/CPB Program.

ANNENBERG/CPB PROGRAM

The Annenberg/CPB Program is a partnership between the Annenberg Foundation and the Corporation for Public Broadcasting (CPB). While the primary purpose of the Annenberg/CPB Program is to use media and telecommunications to promote excellence in teaching in American schools, its educational videos have, for many years, helped college students and military personnel prepare for college credit examinations.

The Annenberg/CPB Program is a valuable educational tool that is well worth the time. Colleges that use videos believe that they enhance and supplement the more traditional instructional methods. Experienced test takers often use the knowledge gained in completing one course or test to prepare for related examinations. Overlapping knowledge is essential to education, and success often requires the use of many resources. The Annenberg/CPB Program is one of these resources. The Annenberg/CPB materials continue to serve as valuable learning tools to supplement knowledge gained through resident courses, independent study courses, or informal learning at home.

Annenberg/CPB Videos

There are over 100 videos available in the Annenberg/CPB series. The videos are grouped according to their subject matter and fall into the following categories:

- Arts
- Child development
- Economics
- Education issues
- Ethics/government
- Geography
- Global studies
- History
- Language
- Literature
- Math
- Psychology/sociology
- Science

Many military education centers keep Annenberg/CPB videos in their library. If the videos are not available at your military education center, you can purchase them by calling (800) LEARNER or ordering over the Internet at *www.learner.org.*

Other Video-Based College Courses
Servicemembers specifically seeking video-based instruction can consult the undergraduate section of the *DANTES External Degree Catalog.* Many of the schools listed in the catalog provide video-based courses. In addition, the *DANTES Independent Study Catalog* lists hundreds of college credit-by-examination courses, many of which offer video-based instruction. In addition to the military education center, most military and civilian libraries have audiovisual materials related to college credit-by-examination topics.

GRADUATE RECORD EXAMINATIONS
Graduate record examinations are designed to assess the comprehensive undergraduate competence of students after four years of college study. There are two types of GRE exams: the general GRE and GRE subject exams.

The general GRE is designed to measure verbal, quantitative, and analytical skills acquired after many years of learning and is generally associated with attendance at a graduate school. These skills are not directly related to any specific field of study.

GRE subject exams measure achievement in specific fields of study, such as knowledge gained in an undergraduate major or mastery of the concepts, principles, and knowledge basic to success in specific graduate fields.

The GRE subject exams are as follows:
- Biochemistry
- Biology
- Chemistry
- Computer science
- Literature in English
- Mathematics
- Physics
- Psychology

All GRE exams are free to servicemembers. However, servicemembers who decide to retake a GRE test to improve their scores must pay for the retest.

College Credit for GRE Exams
Most schools will not award college credit for completion of the general GRE, and it is not covered in this book. Some schools do, however, award

college credit for GRE subject exams. Excelsior College and Thomas Edison State College, for example, will award up to 30 semester hours of college credit in the same subject for successfully completing the corresponding GRE subject exam.

Each school has its own policies governing how much credit it awards for each examination. The most credit that is awarded for any examination, however, is 30 semester hours. Normally, 15 semester hours are granted in both lower-level and upper-level college work. Some schools, like Excelsior College, have implemented a graduated scale so that a student is granted more credit with increased levels of performance on the GRE subject exams. It is likely that all schools will eventually adopt this same graduated-scale approach to granting credit for the GRE subject exams. Although only a high score will result in the awarding of all 30 semester hours, a passing but still below-average score will result in the awarding of at least 3 semester hours. The higher you score, the more semester hours the school will award you.

Scoring of the Tests

GRE subject exams are scored on a scale of 200 to 990 points. The actual range of scores for a particular test is always much smaller, however, because no one ever answers all of the questions correctly. The high scores may be as low as 700. The scores vary widely for each exam, but the scores alone have little meaning without the percentile marks. The percentile mark indicates how well the examinee scored in relation to others who took the same test. A score of 700 may be in the 99th percentile on one GRE subject exam but in the 68th percentile on another.

Administration of GRE Subject Exams

All GRE exams are administered on selected national test dates (usually once per quarter) at most military education centers (see appendix C for the nearest location). Servicemembers must usually make appointments several weeks or months in advance. Since there are limited tests dates in a year and a limit to the number of examinees that the test proctor is allowed to monitor, there is always more demand than supply. When making your schedule, call and check on the next national test date and reserve your seat at the same time.

Additional information can be obtained by contacting GRE at Graduate Record Examination, Educational Testing Service, P.O. Box 6000, Princeton, NJ 08541-6000; phone: (609) 771-7670; Internet website: *www.gre.org*.

12

DANTES Distance Learning Programs

Defense Activity for Non-Traditional Educational Support (DANTES) distance learning is the heart of nontraditional education. It allows servicemembers to take college, technical, and vocational courses from accredited U.S. colleges and universities using textbook reading, online courses, correspondence study, videotapes, computer networks and conferencing, and classes delivered via satellite or cable. DANTES distance learning programs allow servicemembers to take single courses or complete entire degree programs. Using these programs, servicemembers can actually earn an associate, bachelor's, or master's degree, and most require no classroom attendance. These nontraditional programs are perfect for many servicemembers who cannot attend traditional college classes due to work schedules, remote duty locations, and deployments.

PROGRAMS AVAILABLE
There are three different programs available: the DANTES Independent Study Program, the DANTES External Degree Program, and the DANTES Nationally Accredited Distance Learning Program.

DANTES Independent Study Program
The DANTES Independent Study Program allows servicemembers to pursue a variety of individual college courses. *The DANTES Independent Study Catalog* provides servicemembers with more than 6,000 high school, undergraduate, graduate, and examination preparation correspondence courses from which to choose. All of the courses are offered by regionally accredited institutions.

DANTES External Degree Program
The DANTES External Degree Program makes available degree programs from approximately 80 accredited colleges and universities that have few or no residency requirements for degree completion. With this program, servicemembers can earn an Associate of Arts (AA), Associate of Science (AS), Bachelor of Arts (BA), Bachelor of Science (BS), Master of Arts (MA), or Master of Science (MS) degree. The *DANTES External Degree Catalog* lists approximately 100 associate, 225 baccalaureate, and 100 graduate degree programs, as well as about 45 credit-bearing certificate programs. All of the external degree programs are offered by regionally accredited institutions.

DANTES Nationally Accredited Distance Learning Program
The DANTES Nationally Accredited Distance Learning Program allows servicemembers to take vocational, technical, and some nontechnical courses. The *DANTES Catalog of Nationally Accredited Distance Learning Programs* contains course listings from more than twenty schools accredited by various national accrediting bodies and provides a means of independent study for those who want to earn an associate, bachelor's, or master's degree in a vocational program.

SCHOOLS PARTICIPATING IN THESE PROGRAMS
A complete list of schools that participate in these programs follows.

DANTES Independent Study Program Institutions
University of Alabama, *bama.disted.ua.edu*
University of Alaska–Fairbanks, *www.dist-ed.uaf.edu*
University of Arizona, *www.u.arizona.edu*
Arizona State University, *www.asu.edu*
University of Arkansas, *www.uark.edu*
Brigham Young University, *coned.byu.edu/is*
University of California–Berkeley, *www.unex.berkeley.edu*
Embry-Riddle Aeronautical University, *www.ec.erau.edu*
University of Idaho, *www.uidaho.edu*
University of Illinois, *www.conted.uiuc.edu*
Indiana University, *www.extend.indiana.edu*
University of Kansas, *www.kumc.edu/kuce*
University of Kentucky, *www.uky.edu/isp*
University of Minnesota, *www.uc.umn.edu*
University of Mississippi, *www.olemiss.edu*

Mississippi State University, *www.msstate.edu*
University of Missouri, *cdis.missouri.edu*
University of Nebraska–Lincoln, *www.unl.edu/conted*
University of Nevada–Reno, *www.dce.unr.edu*
University of North Carolina, *www.fridaycenter.unc.edu*
University of North Dakota, *www.conted.und.edu*
University of Northern Iowa, *www.uni.edu/contined*
Ohio University, *www.ohiou.edu/independent*
University of Oklahoma, *www.occe.ou.edu*
Oklahoma State University, *www.okstate.edu/education*
Penn State University, *www.outreach.psu.edu/de*
Portland State University, *extended.pdx.edu/istudy*
University of South Carolina, *www.sc.edu/deis/student.services*
University of Southern Mississippi, *www.usm.edu*
Southwest Texas State University, *www.ideal.swt.edu*
Syracuse University, *www.suce.syr.edu*
University of Tennessee, *www.outreach.utk.edu/deis*
Texas Tech University, *www.dce.ttu.edu*
Thomas Edison State College, *www.tesc.edu/*
University of Utah, *www.instudy.utah.edu/*
Utah State University, *www.usu.edu/*
University of Washington, *www.extension.washington.edu/*
Washington State University, *www.eus.wsu.edu/edp/*
The College of West Virginia, *www.cwv.edu/*
Western Kentucky University, *www.wku.edu/*
University of Wisconsin, *learn.wisconsin.edu/*
University of Wyoming, *ses.uwyo.edu/*

DANTES External Degree Program Institutions
University of Alabama, *bama.ua.edu/~iprogs/exd*
University of Alabama (College of Engineering),
    bama.ua.edu/~disted
University of Arkansas (College of Engineering),
    www.engr.uark.edu
Auburn University (College of Engineering),
    www.eng.auburn.edu/department/eop
Baker College Online, *www.baker.edu*
Barton County Community College, *www.bartonline.org*
Bellevue University, *www.bellevue.edu*
Boise State University, *www.idbsu.edu/conted*

University of California–Berkeley, *learn.berkeley.edu*
California State University–Dominguez Hills, *www.csudh.edu*
Capella University, *www.capellauniversity.edu*
Central Maine Tech College, *www.cmtc.net*
Central Michigan University, *www.cel.cmich.edu*
Central Texas College, *www.ctcd.cc.tx.us*
Charter Oak State College, *www.cosc.edu*
University of Cincinnati, *www.uc.edu/cas*
City Colleges of Chicago, *www.ccc.edu*
City University, *www.cityu.edu*
University of Colorado at Colorado Springs, *www.uccs.edu*
Colorado State University, *www.colostate.edu/Depts/CE*
Columbia Union College, *www.cuc.edu*
University of Dallas Graduate School of Management,
    gsmweb.udallas.edu
Defiance College, *www.globaltown.com/dfl*
University of Denver University College, *www.du.edu*
Duquesne University, *coned.duq.edu/mlls/mllsmain.html*
DeVry Institute of Technology, *online.devry.edu*
East Carolina University, *www.sit.ecu.edu*
Embry-Riddle Aeronautical University, *ec.db.erau.edu*
Excelsior College, *www.excelsior.edu*
Florida Institute of Technology, *www.segs.fit.edu*
Fort Hays State University, *www.fhsu.edu/virtual_college*
George Washington University, *www.gwu.edu*
Georgia Institute of Technology, *www.conted.gatech.edu*
Golden Gate University CyberCampus, *cybercampus.ggu.edu*
Governors State University, *www.govst.edu/bog*
Graceland College, *www.gc-outreach.com*
Herkimer County Community College, *www.hcccia.com*
University of Idaho, *www.uidaho.edu/evo*
Indiana Institute of Technology,
    www.indtech.edu/INTech/cnt5/cnt5.html
Indiana University, *www.extend.indiana.edu*
University of Iowa, *www.uiowa.edu/~ccp*
Ivy Tech State College, *ivytech7.cc.in.us/distance-education*
Kansas State University, *www.dce.ksu.edu*
Keller Graduate School of Management, *online.keller.edu*
Liberty University, *www.liberty.edu*
University of Maryland University College, *www.umuc.edu/gsmt*

Mississippi State University, *www.msstate.edu/web/distance.htm*
University of Missouri, *www.mudirect.missouri.edu*
Mount Wachusett Community College, *www.mwcc.mass.edu*
National American University, *www.national.edu*
National Technological University, *www.ntu.edu*
National University, *www.nu.edu*
University of Nebraska–Medical Center,
  www.unmc.edu/AlliedHealth/pa
New Hampshire College, *www.de.nhc.edu*
University of North Dakota, *www.space.edu*
University of Northern Iowa, *www.uni.edu*
Northwestern College, *www.nc.edu*
Nova Southeastern University, *www.nova.edu/cwis/disted*
Ohio University, *www.ohiou.edu/adultlearning*
Penn State University, *www.outreach.psu.edu/de*
University of Phoenix, *www.uophx.edu*
University of Phoenix Online Programs, *www.uophx.edu/online*
Pikes Peak Community College, *www.ppcc.cccoes.edu*
Regent University, *www.regent.edu*
Regis University–External MBA Program, *www.mbaregis.com*
Rochester Institute of Technology, *www.distancelearning.rit.edu*
Roger Williams University, *www.rwu.edu*
Saint Francis College, *www.sfcpa.edu*
Saint Joseph's College, *www.sjcme.edu*
Saint Leo University, *www.saintleo.com*
Salve Regina College, *www.salve.edu*
University of Sarasota, *www.sarasota.edu*
Scott Community College, *eiccd.cc.ia.us/ecat*
Seton Hall University, *www.setonworldwide.net*
Southern Christian University, *www.southernchristian.edu*
University of Southern Colorado, *www.uscolo.edu*
Southern Methodist University, *www.seas.smu.edu*
Strayer University, *www.strayer.edu*
SUNY Empire State College, *www.esc.edu*
Syracuse University, *www.suce.syr.edu/isdp/main*
Texas Tech University, *www.dce.ttu.edu*
Thomas Edison State College, *www.tesc.edu*
Touro University International, *www.tourouniversity.edu*
Troy State University–Alabama, *www.tsulearn.net*
Troy State University–Florida, *www.tsufl.edu*

U.S. Sports Academy, *www.sport.ussa.edu*
Upper Iowa University, *www.uiu.edu*
Vermont College of Norwich University, *www.norwich.edu/vermont-college*
Vincennes University, *www.vinu.edu*
Walden University, *www.waldenu.edu*
Weber State University, *www.weber.edu/distlearn*
The College of West Virginia, *www.cwv.edu*
Western Illinois University, *www.wiu.edu/users/mibogd*

DANTES Nationally Accredited Distance Learning Program Institutions

American Academy of Nutrition, *www.nutritioneducation.com*
American Bible College and Seminary, *www.abcs.edu*
American College of Prehospital Medicine, *www.acpm.edu*
American Graduate University, *www.agu.edu*
American Institute for Computer Sciences, *www.aics.edu*
American Institute of Applied Science, *www.aiasinc.com*
American Military University, *www.amunet.edu*
Andrew Jackson University, *www.aju.edu*
Aviation & Electronics Schools of America, *www.aesa.com*
Berean University, *www.berean.edu*
California College for Health Sciences, *www.cchs.edu*
California National University for Advanced Studies, *www.cnuas.edu*
Catholic Distance University, *www.cdu.edu*
Cleveland Institute of Electronics, *www.cie-wc.edu*
Crown College, *www.crowncollege.edu*
Grantham College of Engineering, *www.grantham.edu*
Harcourt Learning Direct (formerly ICS), *icslearn.com*
ICI University, *www.ici.edu*
ISIM University, *www.isim.edu*
Kaplan College (formerly NIPAS), *www.kaplancollege.com*
University of Leicester, *www.leicester.ac.uk*
Masters Institute, *www.mastersinstitute.edu*
National Tax Training School, *www.nattax.com*
National Training, Inc., *www.truckschool.com*
Rhodec International, *www.rhodec.com*
University of Saint Augustine for Health Sciences, *www.usa.edu*
Travel Lab, *www.boydschool.com*
World College, *www.cie-wc.edu*

HOW COURSES ARE DELIVERED

Schools participating in these programs use a variety of methods to deliver educational choices aimed at individual students around the world. Some schools still offer traditional correspondence study delivered by mail or e-mail, but many schools have capitalized on the latest technologies to offer courses that can be completed entirely over the Internet. Using web-based classroom software, students can submit assignments and receive grades. Instant messaging and web-based class chatrooms allow students to communicate with teachers and fellow students and participate in real-time class discussions. With full multimedia audio and video, students can access course presentations or lectures online. Of course, students still use traditional textbooks, pens, and paper, but many are now using the speed and efficiency of advancing technologies to increase their educational opportunities and decrease both course and degree completion times.

USE OF PROGRAMS

Personnel in all military services are eligible to use the programs and courses offered through the DANTES distance learning programs.

These programs are designed to meet the needs of military personnel who have an educational goal and are willing to work for it. These programs were not designed for those who lack discipline and persistence. Those who succeed in these programs have academic and emotional maturity, specific educational goals, the ability to work alone, the capacity for self-starting, self-understanding, self-motivation, persistence, and self-confidence.

Benefits of Using Programs

With these programs, servicemembers can earn credit wherever they are stationed. These programs are approved for tuition assistance, and, like all programs detailed in this book, they can enhance promotion potential, assist in retirement preparation, and lead to better-paying jobs with higher incomes.

PROGRAM ENROLLMENT

Before enrolling, check with the school; some courses or degree programs have prerequisites or other requirements that must be met prior to enrolling.

To enroll, make an appointment with a counselor at your local military education center. The education counselor will ask about your educational goals and assist you with selecting the appropriate courses to pursue them. These counselors have valuable experience, knowledge, and access to materials that can be helpful in choosing the appropriate school. The counselor will then help you complete the *DANTES Distance Learning Enrollment Form* (DANTES 1562/31). Mail the first two copies, signed by you and your counselor or other certifying official, with the total payment or credit card number (to cover tuition, fees, and book costs) directly to the school. DANTES will reimburse you only if this form is used. Some schools also require students to complete the school enrollment form.

The only limits to how many courses you take are those that you impose on yourself, but be realistic. Education counselors normally recommend one course to start, until you get your feet wet. There may also be budget constraints that dictate how many courses for which you can be reimbursed. Listen to your education counselor.

TUITION AND OTHER FEES

Depending on budget requirements of that fiscal year, possible specified dollar limits, and availability of funding, servicemembers are reimbursed 75 percent of the tuition costs. No lab, special, textbook, or postage fees are reimbursed. Servicemembers pay postage for materials sent to the distance learning school; the school pays postage on materials sent to the servicemembers. Servicemembers should always speak with their counselors to clarify current tuition assistance funding levels before registering for a course. Unlike other college courses, servicemembers must pay all distance learning costs at enrollment. After successfully completing the course, servicemembers will be reimbursed.

Payment

Some schools have plans that allow for installment payments. These plans are an agreement between the student and the school. The student must pay all costs before the school will issue a grade report, and tuition reimbursement cannot be made until the school issues a grade report. If you are considering enrolling, be sure to ask the school about refund policies before enrolling or before signing a contract. Most schools also permit payment by credit card. When paying by credit card, use the space for the card number on the *DANTES Distance Learning Enrollment Form*, and be sure the school accepts the type of credit card you are using.

Reimbursement

DANTES will process the reimbursement upon successful completion of the course for schools listed in the DANTES catalogs. The school will send DANTES a grade report, usually within 30 days of the course completion. Upon receipt of the grade report, DANTES processes the application, and the servicemember is reimbursed by DANTES or his or her respective service.

13

Excelsior College

Excelsior College, formerly known as Regents College, is one of the best-known and most utilized nontraditional postsecondary institutions in the United States. It participates in DANTES. Excelsior maintains that "what someone knows is more important than where and how the knowledge was acquired." Excelsior College provides the opportunity for motivated adult learners to obtain recognition of their college-level educational achievement. Excelsior College is also one of the oldest and largest assessment and evaluation institutions in the United States. It works in active partnership with colleges and universities, employers, healthcare institutions, the U.S. military, and other organizations throughout the country to provide access to an affordable higher-education experience. While maintaining a liberal admissions policy, Excelsior College assures academic integrity through rigorous requirements and a careful assessment process.

HOW EXCELSIOR COLLEGE WORKS

Excelsior College offers thirty associate and bachelor's degrees in business, liberal arts, nursing, and technology; two master's degrees in liberal studies and nursing; and two certificate programs in nursing. The college has no campus residency requirement. When students enroll, their prior college-level learning, both traditional classroom learning and many types of nontraditional learning, is evaluated for credit. The students then work with assigned academic advisors by phone, mail, and e-mail to determine the best route to completing their degrees. Students can complete degree requirements through a wide variety of methods, including traditional college courses, accredited distance learning courses, military training and courses, selected on-the-job training, and accredited examinations for college credit. All of these experiences are evaluated and consolidated on a single transcript.

ACCREDITATION
Excelsior College is accredited by the Middle States Association of Colleges and Schools. The associate and baccalaureate degree programs in nursing at Excelsior College are accredited by the National League for Nursing Accrediting Commission. The baccalaureate degree programs in electronics engineering technology and nuclear engineering technology are accredited by the Technology Accreditation Commission of the Accreditation Board for Engineering and Technology.

STUDENTS
Many Excelsior College graduates are people just like you: military personnel, working adults, or those with no access to traditional college resources. Excelsior College has students who live in every state in the United States and in many foreign countries. Thousands of students graduate from Excelsior every year, and the college has awarded nearly 100,000 degrees. Nearly three-quarters of Excelsior's graduates expect to earn a master's or higher degree in their lifetime, and nearly 40 percent of the baccalaureate graduates pursue postgraduate study immediately after earning their Excelsior College degree. The vast majority of Excelsior College students are working adults employed full-time.

DEGREES AND PROGRAMS
Excelsior College offers associate, bachelor's, and master's degrees in four programs: business, liberal arts, nursing, and technology and engineering. Among other requirements, each associate degree requires 60 semester hours, each bachelor's degree requires 120 semester hours, and each master's degree requires approximately 30 semester hours beyond the bachelor's degree. The following degrees are offered by Excelsior College:

Business Degrees
Associate of Applied Science in Administrative/Management Studies
Associate of Science (Business)
Bachelor of Science in Accounting (General)
Bachelor of Science in Accounting (New York State CPA Track)
Bachelor of Science in Finance
Bachelor of Science in General Business
Bachelor of Science in International Business
Bachelor of Science in Management of Human Resources
Bachelor of Science in Management Information Systems
Bachelor of Science in Marketing
Bachelor of Science in Operations Management

Liberal Arts Degrees
Associate of Arts
Associate of Science
Bachelor of Arts (students can satisfy the 120-semester-hour requirement via a liberal studies option, which includes two depth requirements of 12 semester credits each, or a concentration option, which includes a concentration of 30 semester credits and a depth requirement of 12 semester hours)
Bachelor of Science (students can satisfy the 120-semester-hour requirement via a liberal studies option, which includes two depth requirements of 12 semester credits each, or a concentration option, which includes a concentration of 30 semester credits and a depth requirement of 12 semester hours)
Students may pursue one the following concentrations as part of both the BS and BA degrees:
Area Studies (e.g., Middle East, Latin America)
Biology
Chemistry
Communication
Economics
Geography
Geology
History
Literature in English
Mathematics
Music
Philosophy
Physics
Political Science
Psychology
Sociology
World Language and Literature
Master of Arts in Liberal Studies (requires 33 semester hours of graduate-level credit in the arts and sciences and a thesis, among other requirements)

Nursing Degrees
Associate of Applied Science (Nursing)
Associate of Science (Nursing)
Bachelor of Science (Nursing)
Master of Science (Nursing)

Technology and Engineering Degrees
Associate of Applied Science in Aviation Studies
Associate of Applied Science in Technical Studies
Associate of Occupational Studies in Aviation
Associate of Science in Computer Software
Associate of Science in Electronics Technology
Associate of Science in Nuclear Technology
Associate of Science in Technology
Bachelor of Science in Computer Information Systems
Bachelor of Science in Computer Technology
Bachelor of Science in Electronics Engineering Technology
Bachelor of Science in Nuclear Engineering Technology
Bachelor of Science in Technology

Suitability for Servicemembers

To accommodate the needs of servicemembers, Excelsior College participates in the Army University Access Online Program and the Servicemembers Opportunity Colleges Program. Excelsior has also developed its own military degrees for Army, Navy, Marine Corps, and Coast Guard personnel. As a member of the Servicemembers Opportunity Colleges (SOC) Program, Excelsior College offers military personnel the benefits of liberal credit transfer policies, minimum residency requirements, acceptance of extrainstitutional learning, and maximized transfer credit. The Servicemembers Opportunity Colleges Program is covered in detail in chapter 15.

The Army portion of these degrees forms Excelsior's contribution to the Army University Access Online Program (eArmyU). While the eArmyU was designed specifically for Army personnel, the four associate degrees offered by Excelsior College under this program are also available to Navy, Marine Corps, and Coast Guard personnel. Additionally, Excelsior College's other associate and bachelor's degrees, especially the liberal arts degrees, are very popular with servicemembers.

While Excelsior College does not offer programs specifically designed for Air Force Specialty Codes, Air Force personnel are eligible to pursue any military degree program offered by Excelsior College. As a rule, Air Force education officers and Excelsior College strongly encourage Air Force personnel to complete their associate degrees with the Community College of the Air Force since those programs offer the maximize benefit for Air Force personnel. Nevertheless, Air Force personnel may apply their CCAF credits toward any of Excelsior's associate degree programs linked to the Army, Navy, Coast Guard, and Marine career fields.

All servicemembers, whether they are Air Force, Army, Navy, or Marine Corps, are eligible to pursue any of Excelsior's bachelor's or master's degree programs in business, liberal arts, nursing, and technology and engineering.

Army University Access Online Program (eArmyU)

Excelsior College was one of the first schools to participate in the Army University Access Online (AUAO) Program. This program enables U.S. enlisted soldiers to obtain professional technical certifications and associate, bachelor's, and master's degrees using laptop computers to access online courses while they serve in the Army. Upon their initial enrollment, soldiers participating in this program are issued a laptop computer to access their courses. They also receive a printer, Internet access, and technical support, accessible online and over the telephone. Through the Army University Access Online Program, the following degrees are available:

Associate of Applied Science in Administrative/Management Studies

Associate of Applied Science in Aviation Studies

Associate of Applied Science in Technical Studies

Associate of Occupational Studies in Aviation

To learn more about the Army University Access Online Program, see chapter 4, contact the Army education counselor, or go to *www.-earmyu.com.*

Excelsior's Military Degrees

Below is a list of degrees that Excelsior College developed for the military:

Associate of Applied Science in Administrative/Management Studies: This degree is designed specifically for military personnel and is suited for the following career fields:

Army military occupational specialties (MOSs): 00Z, 11B, 11C, 11H, 11M, 11Z, 13B, 13C, 13D, 13E, 13M, 13P, 13R, 13T, 13Z, 14D, 14J, 14L, 14M, 14R, 14S, 18B, 18D, 18E, 18F, 18Z, 19D, 19K, 19Z, 25Z, 37F, 38A, 43M, 57E, 71D, 71G, 71L, 71M, 73C, 73D, 73Z, 75B, 75F, 75H, 76J, 79R, 79S, 79T, 88H, 88K, 88M, 88N, 88X, 88Z, 91B, 91M, 92A, 92G, 92M, 92R, 92Y, 92Z, 93C, 93F, 93P, 95B, 95C, 95D, 96B, 96D, 96H, 98J, 98K, 98Z, and corresponding warrant officer MOSs

Navy ratings: AC, AK, AZ, BM, CTA, CTI, CTO, CTR, DK, IS, LN, MA, MS, NC, PC, PN, QM, RP, SH, SK, SM, YN, and corresponding warrant officer and limited duty officer ratings

Marine Corps MOSs: 0151, 0161, 0231, 0311, 0321, 0331, 0332, 0341, 0351, 0352, 0369, 0811, 0842, 0844, 0861, 1171, 1181, 1811, 1812, 2621, 2629, 2631, 2643, 2651, 2671, 2673, 2674, 2675, 3043, 3044, 3112, 3381, 3421, 3451, 3529, 3533, 3537, 4421, 5811, 5812, 5831, 6391, 6591, 7041, 7324, 8431, 8611, 8915

Coast Guard ratings: BM, IV, PS, QM, RD, SK, SS, TC, YN, and corresponding warrant officer ratings

Associate of Applied Science in Aviation Studies: This degree is designed for Army and Coast Guard aviators.

Associate of Applied Science in Technical Studies (with the chemical technologies specialty): This degree is suited for enlisted servicemembers in Army MOSs 54B, 77F, 77L, and 77W and related warrant officer MOSs

Associate of Applied Science in Technical Studies (with the computer technologies specialty): This degree is suited for enlisted servicemembers in the following career fields:

Army MOSs: 74B, 74C, 74G, 74Z, and related warrant officer MOSs

Navy ratings: DS, IS, and related warrant officer and limited duty officer ratings

Marine Corps MOS: 4069

Coast Guard ratings: DP and related warrant officer ratings

Associate of Applied Science in Technical Studies (with the electromechanical technologies specialty): This degree is suited for enlisted servicemembers in the following career fields:

Army MOSs: 12B 12C, 12Z, 14E, 14T, 23R, 24H, 24K, 27E, 27G, 27H, 27K, 27M, 27T, 27X, 27Z, 44B, 44E, 45B, 45D, 45E, 45G, 45K, 45N, 45T, 51B, 51H, 51K, 51M, 51R, 51T, 51Z, 52C, 52D, 52E, 52G, 52X, 55B, 55D, 62B, 62E, 62F, 62G, 62H, 62J, 62N, 63B, 63D, 63E, 63G, 63H, 63J, 63N, 63S, 63T, 63W, 63Y, 63Z, 67G, 67N, 67R, 67S, 67T, 67U, 67V, 67Y, 67Z, 68B, 68D, 68F, 68G, 68H, 68J, 68K, 68N, 68X, 88L, 88P, 88T, and corresponding warrant officer MOSs

Navy ratings: AB, AD, AE, AF, AM, AO, AS, AT, AV, BT, BU CE, CM CU, DC, EA, EM, EN, EO, EQ, ET, FC, FT, GM, GS, HT,

IC, IM, MM, MN, MR, MT, OM, PR, SW, UC, UT, and corresponding warrant officer and limited duty officer ratings

Marine Corps MOSs: 1141, 1345, 1371, 2111, 2311, 2336, 3521, 3522, 3524, 5923, 5929, 5994, 6013, 6014, 6015, 6016, 6017, 6019, 6022, 6025, 6026, 6027, 6035, 6043, 6044, 6053, 6055, 6056, 6057, 6058, 6060, 6072, 6073, 6075, 6083, 6085, 6086, 6087, 6092, 6094, 6112, 6113, 6114, 6115, 6119, 6122, 6123, 6124, 6125, 6132, 6135, 6152, 6153, 6154, 6155, 6172, 6173, 6174, 6175, 6176, 6386, 6462, 6463, 6464, 6465, 6466, 6467, 6468, 6469, 6482, 6483, 6484, 6485, 6492, 6494, 6521, 6531, 6541

Coast Guard ratings: AD, AE, AM, AMT, ASM, AT, DC, EM, ET, FT, GM, MK, and corresponding warrant officer ratings

Associate of Applied Science in Technical Studies (with the electronic/instrumentation technologies specialty): This degree is suited for enlisted servicemembers in the following career fields:

Army MOSs: 25R, 31C, 31F, 31L, 31P, 31R, 31S, 31U, 31W, 31Z, 33W, 35B, 35C, 35D, 35E, 35F, 35H, 35J, 35L, 35M, 35N, 35Q, 35R, 35W, 35Y, 35Z, 39B, 39G, 81T, 81Z, 82C, 82D, 91A, and corresponding warrant officer MOSs

Navy ratings: AW, CTM, CTT, EW, OS, OT, ST, and corresponding warrant officer and limited duty officer ratings

Marine Corps MOSs: 2512, 2531, 2534, 2831, 2841, 6313, 6314, 6315, 6316, 6317, 6322, 6323, 6324, 6325, 6412, 6316, 6317, 6322, 6323, 6324, 6325, 6412, 6413, 6414, 6422, 6423, 6432, 6433, 6434

Coast Guard ratings: AVT, ST, TT, and related warrant officer ratings

Associate of Applied Science in Technical Studies (with the nuclear technologies specialty): This degree is suited for enlisted servicemembers in Navy ratings EM, ET, IC, and MM (for those with nuclear power training) and corresponding warrant officer and limited duty officer ratings

Cost of Earning a Degree

The cost of pursuing a degree through Excelsior College varies, depending on the degree and how long it takes a student to complete the degree. Excelsior also offers special tuition rates for military personnel. The fees normally

increase modestly each year, but Excelsior remains one of the most affordable nontraditional schools available to servicemembers. Students can obtain
a specific tuition and fee schedule from Excelsior College's website:
www.excelsior.edu.

To obtain more information about Excelsior College degrees, call
Excelsior College at (518) 464-8500 or visit the Excelsior College website:
www.excelsior.edu. If you prefer, you can write to Excelsior College, 7
Columbia Circle, Albany, NY 12203-5159.

14

Thomas Edison State College

Thomas Edison State College, like Excelsior College, is one of the best known and most utilized nontraditional postsecondary institutions in the United States. It, too, is a DANTES participant. The mission of the school provides "diverse and alternative methods of achieving a collegiate education of the highest quality for mature adults." Thomas Edison State College claims that it is entirely devoted to the adult learner. The school is named after Thomas Alva Edison, who achieved college-level knowledge through independent research. Using distance education, Thomas Edison enables adult learners to complete associate, bachelor's, and master's degrees wherever they live and work. Students in any state or nation can earn credit for college-level knowledge acquired outside the classroom, and Thomas Edison State College has *no residency requirements.*

HOW THOMAS EDISON STATE COLLEGE WORKS
Upon enrollment, Thomas Edison State College (TESC) students transfer an average of 30 to 60 semester hours to the school from other sources. After a student applies to a particular degree program, TESC assesses his or her learning and experiences and determines how close the student is to completing the desired degree. The student then enrolls and selects his or her preferred method or methods of completing the degree requirements. In addition to other nontraditional sources of college credit, there are several unique degree completion options at TESC, including portfolio assessment, guided study, an online computer classroom, contract learning courses, the Thomas Edison State College examination program, e-Pack, and independent study pack courses.

ACCREDITATION

Thomas Edison State College is accredited by the Commission on Higher Education of the Middle States Association of Colleges and Schools. The Thomas Edison State College Nursing Program is accredited by the National League for Nursing.

STUDENTS

TESC has awarded thousands of degrees to students worldwide, and it is designed exclusively for adult learners. While most of TESC's students are residents of New Jersey, many come from other states and foreign countries.

DEGREES AND PROGRAMS

TESC offers seven associate and six bachelor's degrees in over 100 different areas of study, and it offers two master's degrees. Among other requirements, each associate degree requires 60 semester hours, each bachelor's degree requires 120 semester hours, and each master's degree requires approximately 30 semester hours beyond the bachelor's degree. The following degrees are offered by Thomas Edison State College:

Associate of Applied Science
Associate of Applied Science in Radiologic Technology
Associate of Arts
Associate of Science in Applied Science and Technology
Associate of Science in Management
Associate of Science in Natural Sciences and Mathematics
Associate of Science in Public and Social Services
Bachelor of Arts
Bachelor of Science in Applied Science and Technology
Bachelor of Science in Business Administration
Bachelor of Science in Health Sciences
Bachelor of Science in Human Services
Bachelor of Science in Nursing
Master of Arts in Professional Studies
Master of Science in Management

Liberal Arts Degrees

The Associate of Arts degree requires 60 semester hours of credit, among other requirements. The Associate of Science degree in Natural Sciences and Mathematics requires 60 semester hours of credit, among other requirements. Students may pursue studies in biology, chemistry, computer science, mathematics, or physics.

The Bachelor of Arts degree requires 120 semester hours of credit, among other requirements. Students may select between an area concentration, a liberal studies option, or an area of study major. The area concentration requires 33 semester hours in three different liberal arts subject areas (humanities, social sciences/history, or natural sciences/mathematics). The liberal studies option requires 33 semester hours in two or more liberal arts subject areas. The area of study major requires 33 semester hours in a single subject area.

Bachelor of Arts degree subject areas follow:

Humanities
Art
Communications
English
Foreign language
Journalism
Music
Philosophy
Photography
Religion
Theater arts

Social Sciences/History
Anthropology
Economics
History
Labor studies
Political science
Psychology
Sociology

Natural Sciences/Mathematics
Biology
Chemistry
Computer science
Mathematics
Physics

Interdisciplinary
Environmental studies

A Master of Arts degree in Professional Studies is also offered. It requires 36 semester hours of graduate-level credit, among other requirements.

Business and Management Degrees

The Associate of Science in Management degree requires 60 semester hours of credit, among other requirements. Students may pursue one of the following specializations:

> Accounting
> Administrative office management
> Banking
> Computer information systems
> Finance
> General management
> Hospital healthcare administration
> Hotel/motel/restaurant management
> Human resources management
> Insurance
> International business
> Marketing
> Operations management
> Procurement
> Public administration
> Purchasing and materials management
> Real estate
> Retailing management
> Small business management/entrepreneurship
> Transportation/distribution management

The Bachelor of Science in Business Administration requires 120 semester hours of credit, which includes a specialization, among other requirements. Students may pursue one of the following specializations (18 semester hours in one subject area):

> Accounting
> Administrative office management
> Advertising management
> Banking
> Computer information systems
> Finance
> General management

Hospital healthcare administration
Hotel/motel/restaurant management
Human resources management
Insurance
International business
Logistics
Marketing
Operations management
Organizational management
Procurement
Public administration
Purchasing and materials management
Real estate
Retailing management
Small business management/entrepreneurship
Transportation/distribution management

The Master of Science in Management requires 36 semester hours of graduate-level credit, among other requirements. Students may pursue leadership, project management, or management of substance abuse programs.

Nursing and Health Sciences Degrees
The Bachelor of Science in Health Sciences degree requires 120 semester hours of credit, among other requirements. This is a joint degree program with the University of Medicine and Dentistry of New Jersey School of Health Related Professions and is designed for students (including military students) who are already in the allied health field. Students may pursue one of the following concentrations:
Advanced practice with tracks in:
Advanced dental assisting sciences
Advanced dental hygiene sciences
Advanced respiratory care sciences
Dietetic sciences
Imaging sciences
Health professions education
Health services management

The Bachelor of Science in Nursing degree requires 120 semester hours of credit, among other requirements, but it is available only to registered nurses living or working in New Jersey.

Applied Science and Technology Degrees

An Associate of Science in Applied Science degree requires 60 semester hours of credit, among other requirements. Students may choose administrative studies, applied electronic studies, applied health studies, mechanics and maintenance, or occupational studies.

The Associate of Science in Applied Science and Technology degree also requires 60 semester hours of credit, among other requirements. Students may pursue one of the following specializations:

Air traffic control*
Architectural design
Aviation flight technology*
Aviation maintenance technology*
Biomedical electronics
Civil and construction engineering technology
Clinical laboratory science*
Computer science technology
Dental hygiene*
Electrical technology
Electronics engineering technology
Engineering graphics
Environmental sciences
Fire protection science
Forestry
Horticulture
Laboratory animal science
Manufacturing engineering technology
Marine engineering technology
Mechanical engineering technology
Nondestructive testing technology
Nuclear engineering technology
Nuclear medicine technology*
Radiation protection
Radiation therapy*
Respiratory care*
Surveying

*Students enrolled in these specializations must already hold a professional certification.

An Associate of Applied Science in Radiologic Technology is also available from Thomas Edison State College. It requires 60 semester hours, among other requirements.

The Bachelor of Science in Applied Science and Technology requires 120 semester hours of credit, which includes a specialization, among other requirements. Students may pursue one of the following specializations (33 semester hours in one area):

Air traffic control*
Architectural design
Aviation flight technology*
Aviation maintenance technology*
Biomedical electronics
Civil engineering technology
Clinical laboratory science*
Computer science technology
Construction
Cytotechnology*
Dental hygiene*
Electrical technology
Electronics engineering technology
Engineering graphics
Environmental sciences
Fire protection science
Forestry
Horticulture
Laboratory animal science
Manufacturing engineering technology
Marine engineering technology
Mechanical engineering technology
Medical imaging*
Nondestructive testing technology
Nuclear engineering technology
Nuclear medicine technology*
Perfusion technology*
Radiation protection
Radiation therapy*
Respiratory care*
Surveying

*Students enrolled in these specializations must already hold a professional certification.

Human and Social Services Degrees

The Associate of Science in Public and Social Services degree requires 60 semester hours of credit, among other requirements. Students may pursue one of the following specializations:

Administration of justice
Child development services
Community services
Emergency disaster management
Gerontology
Legal services
Recreation services
Social services
Social services for special populations

The Bachelor of Science in Human Services degree requires 120 semester hours of credit, which includes a specialization, among other requirements. Students may pursue one of the following specializations (33 semester hours in one area):

Administration of justice
Child development services
Community services
Emergency disaster management
Gerontology
Health and nutrition counseling
Health services
Health services administration
Health services education
Legal services
Mental health and rehabilitative services
Recreation services
Social services
Social services administration
Social services for special populations

Suitability for Servicemembers

To accommodate the needs of servicemembers, TESC participates in four programs developed specifically for military personnel: the Military Degree Completion Program, the Army University Access Online Program, the Navy College Partnership Program, and the Servicemembers Opportunity Colleges Program.

Military Degree Completion Program

Air Force, Army, Navy, and Marine Corps personnel are eligible to participate in this program, which uses innovative instructional approaches rather than classroom-based courses. It is ideal for military personnel who need 12 semester hours or more to complete their degree. Each degree offered has a program of study defined by a personal academic program plan in which military training, previous college credit, and licensure and certifications may be used to satisfy TESC requirements. Your academic plan maps out your degree with a profile of credit-earning options that can help you satisfy your degree requirements. The following degrees are offered as part of the Military Degree Completion Program:

Associate Degrees

Associate of Applied Science (major matches your military occupation):
  Administrative studies
  Applied computer studies
  Applied electronic studies
  Applied health studies
  Mechanics and maintenance
  Occupational studies
Associate of Applied Science in Radiologic Technology[*]
Associate of Arts
Associate of Science in Applied Science and Technology[*]
Associate of Science in Management (major in general management)
Associate of Science in Public and Social Services[*]

Baccalaureate Degrees

Bachelor of Arts (major in liberal studies, social sciences, humanities, or psychology)
Bachelor of Science in Applied Science and Technology[*]
Bachelor of Science in Business Administration General Management
Bachelor of Science in Human Services[*]

[*]Students may only pursue majors in these degrees that correspond to their military occupation.

Army University Access Online Program (eArmyU)

TESC was one of the first schools to participate in the Army University Access Online (AUAO) Program. This program enables U.S. enlisted soldiers to obtain professional technical certifications and associate, bachelor's, and master's degrees using laptop computers to access online courses while they serve in the Army. Upon their initial enrollment, soldiers participating in this program are issued a laptop computer to access their courses. They also receive a printer, Internet access, and technical support accessible, online and over the telephone. The following degrees are available through the Army University Access Online Program, (eArmyU):

Associate of Science in Applied Science and Technology
Associate of Science in Management
Bachelor of Arts
Master of Arts in Professional Studies
Master of Science in Management

To learn more about the Army University Access Online Program, see chapter 4, contact the Army education counselor, or go to *www.earmyu.com*.

Navy College Partnership Program

Thomas Edison State College offers sailors the opportunity to seek a degree through the Navy College Partnership Program. All Navy college students are provided with an academic program evaluation when they apply to the college. With this evaluation students work with an advisor to develop a program plan that maps out the courses, exams, and military training they need to complete their remaining degree requirements. This program plan also helps students to develop a timeline for completion of their degree. TESC offers courses in six 16-week terms and one eight-week term each year. TESC's six 16-week terms overlap so that servicemembers have greater flexibility in building their academic schedules. Students must complete at least 6 semester hours toward an associate degree at TESC and 12 semester hours toward a bachelor's degree to meet residency requirements. The following Navy ratings and corresponding degrees are included in the Navy College Program:

AC Air Traffic Controller
Associate of Science in Applied Science and Technology (ASAST): Air Traffic Control
Bachelor of Science in Applied Science and Technology (BSAST): Air Traffic Control
AD Aviation Machinist's Mate
AAS in Mechanics and Maintenance: Aviation Maintenance
AE Aviation Electrician's Mate
AAS in Applied Electronic Studies: Electrician

AG Aerographer
  AA: Meteorology
  BA: Natural Science
BU Builder
  AAS in Occupational Studies: Building
CE Construction Electrician
  AAS in Applied Electronic Studies: Electrician
CM Construction Mechanic
  AAS in Mechanics and Maintenance: Mechanics
CTI Cryptologic Technician (Interpretive)
  AA: General Studies
  BA: Humanities
CTM Cryptologic Technician (Maintenance)
  AAS in Applied Electronic Studies: Electronic Studies
DT Dental Assistant
  AAS in Applied Health Studies: Dental Assistant
EM Electrician's Mate
  AAS in Applied Electronic Studies: Electrician
GSE Gas Turbine System Technician (Electrical)
  AAS in Applied Electronic Studies: Electrician
EM(NUC) Electrician's Mate Nuclear
  ASAST: Nuclear Engineering Technology
  BSAST: Nuclear Engineering Technology
ET Electronic Technician
  AAS in Applied Electronic Studies: Electronic Studies
ET(NUC) Electronics Technician Nuclear
  ASAST: Nuclear Engineering Technology
  BSAST: Nuclear Engineering Technology
EW Electronic Warfare Technician
  AAS in Applied Electronic Studies: Electronic Studies
FT Fire Control Technician
  AAS in Applied Electronic Studies: Electronic Studies, Surface
  AAS in Applied Electronic Studies: Electronic Studies, Submarine
GM Gunner's Mate
  AAS in Mechanics and Maintenance: Mechanics
IC Interior Communications Electrician
  AAS in Applied Electronic Studies: Electronic Studies
MM(NUC) Machinist's Mate Nuclear
  ASAST: Nuclear Engineering Technology
  BSAST: Nuclear Engineering Technology

MT Missile Technician
   AAS in Applied Electronic Studies: Electronic Studies
MU Musician
   AA: Music
   BA: Humanities
PH Photographer's Mate
   AA: Photography
RP Religious Program Specialist
   AAS in Administrative Studies

Servicemembers Opportunity Colleges Program

As a member of the Servicemembers Opportunity Colleges (SOC) Program, TESC offers military personnel the benefits of liberal credit transfer policies, no residency requirements, acceptance of extrainstitutional learning, and maximized transfer credit. Although TESC does not offer programs specifically developed for the Air Force, attending TESC through the SOC program is especially useful to Air Force personnel who have completed their associate degree with CCAF and wish to continue their education and complete a bachelor's degree. The Servicemembers Opportunity Colleges Program is covered in detail in chapter 15. Although TESC does not offer programs specifically developed for the Air Force, attending TESC through the SOC program is especially useful to Air Force personnel who have completed their associate's degree with CCAF and wish to continue their education and complete a bachelor's degree.

Cost of Earning a Degree

The cost of pursuing a degree through Thomas Edison State College varies, depending on factors such as the number of credits being transferred and the methods used to complete the remaining degree requirements. Generally, the more college a student has completed before enrolling, the less that student will pay to complete the desired degree. TESC does offer tuition rates geared specifically for servicemembers. Since tuition rates are raised periodically and vary by program, students should contact the school to obtain a specific fee schedule.

To obtain more information about Thomas Edison State College, call the TESC Office of Admissions Services at (888) 442-8372, e-mail TESC at *info@tesc.edu*, or visit the TESC website: *www.tesc.edu*. If you prefer, you can write to Thomas Edison State College, 101 West State Street, Trenton, NJ 08608-1176.

15

Servicemembers
Opportunity Colleges

Servicemembers Opportunity Colleges are colleges and universities that have developed special policies and procedures for military personnel that make it easier for them to earn college degrees. In 1972, these colleges, in cooperation with the Department of Defense, the military services—and one another—formed what is known today as the Servicemembers Opportunity Colleges (SOC) Program. The SOC Program comprises a network of over 1,500 colleges and universities. The special policies and procedures of these colleges apply only to their military college students; their civilian college students still must pursue their degrees via the more tedious, more expensive traditional routes. By granting college credit for knowledge gained through nontraditional methods, minimizing the residency requirements, and maximizing the amount of credit allowed for transfer, these schools make it easier for servicemembers to earn associate and bachelor's degrees.

HOW THE SOC PROGRAM HELPS SERVICEMEMBERS
The SOC Program helps servicemembers save money and earn their degrees faster. The transfer practices of SOC Program schools allow servicemembers to minimize college credit lost in transfer, thus avoiding duplication of course work. These schools limit their residency requirements for military personnel to 25 percent of the undergraduate degree program. A school also agrees to accept any course taken at that institution during the SOC agreement period as credit toward the school residency requirement. These policies help servicemembers avoid the need to take extra courses to meet residency requirements. SOC schools have agreed to award college credit for a servicemember's military training and experiences when those credits apply toward the degree being sought. Finally, SOC schools have processes to evaluate and award college credit for nationally recognized extrainstitutional learning,

such as CLEP examinations, the DANTES Subject Standardized Test (DSST), and the Excelsior College Examination (ECE).

HOW THE SOC PROGRAM WORKS

After seeing an education counselor and selecting an SOC school offering the desired degree, a servicemember speaks with a school representative and requests an unofficial evaluation of his or her college work and experiences. To request an evaluation, servicemembers must normally request that a transcript from AARTS, SMART, or CCAF or a DD Form 295 or 2586 (VMET) be forwarded to the school. Using the evaluation as a guide, the servicemember will complete at least 6 semester hours of course work (which is normally two classes) toward the selected degree program. The official SOC agreement is then signed by the school and the student. The agreement guarantees that the servicemember can earn his or her degree with that institution as long as he or she completes 25 percent of his credits at that school. The remaining degree requirements can be completed at the same college or at any one of the over 1,500 schools that have agreed to abide by the rules of the SOC Program. It does not matter how often the servicemember transfers or how many different colleges he or she attends, because the contract is a guarantee. Once the degree requirements are met, the school that signed the SOC agreement will award the degree to the servicemember.

ACCREDITATION

All Servicemembers Opportunity Colleges are fully accredited. In order to be a member of the SOC Program, a school must be a degree-granting institution that is accredited by an institutional accrediting agency recognized by the Council on Postsecondary Accreditation.

DEGREES

The full range of associate, baccalaureate, and graduate degrees is awarded by member schools of the SOC Program. Degrees in nearly every major imaginable are available through SOC member schools. Servicemembers should check with nearby SOC schools to determine the availability of specific degree programs.

Cost of Earning a Degree

The SOC agreement is free. Of course, all institutions charge their own tuition rates for courses required to complete the degree requirements. Be sure to request an unofficial evaluation of your college credit and military experiences before taking any classes.

Schools Participating in the SOC Program
All SOC schools are listed below:

Alabama
Alabama Agricultural and Mechanical University
Alabama Southern Community College
Andrew Jackson University
Athens State University
Auburn University at Montgomery
Bevill State Community College
Bishop State Community College
Calhoun Community College
Central Alabama Community College
Chattahoochee Valley Community College
Enterprise State Junior College
Faulkner State Community College
Faulkner University
Gadsden State Community College
George C. Wallace State Community College–Dothan
Harry M. Ayers State Technical College
Herzing College
Huntingdon College
J. F. Drake State Technical College
Jacksonville State University
Jefferson Davis Community College
Jefferson State Community College
Judson College
Lawson State Community College
Lurleen B. Wallace Junior College
Northeast Alabama Community College
Northwest-Shoals Community College
Oakwood College
Reid State Technical College
Shelton State Community College
Snead State Community College
South College
Southeast College of Technology
Southern Christian University
Southern Union State Community College
Talladega College
Trenholm State Technical College

Troy State University
Troy State University Dothan
Troy State University Montgomery
United States Sports Academy
University of Alabama at Birmingham
University of Alabama at Tuscaloosa
University of Alabama in Huntsville
University of Mobile
University of Montevallo
University of North Alabama
University of South Alabama
University of West Alabama
Virginia College at Birmingham
Wallace Community College–Selma
Wallace State Community College–Hanceville

Alaska
Alaska Pacific University
University of Alaska Anchorage
University of Alaska Fairbanks
University of Alaska Southeast

American Samoa
American Samoa Community College

Arizona
Arizona Institute of Business and Technology
Arizona Western College
Central Arizona College
Cochise College
Gate Way Community College
Glendale Community College
Grand Canyon University
ITT Technical Institute–Phoenix Campus
Mesa Community College
Mohave Community College
Paradise Valley Community College
Phoenix College
Pima County Community College
Prescott College

Rio Salado College
Scottsdale Community College
University of Advancing Computer Technology
University of Arizona–Extended University and University Arizona,
    South
University of Phoenix
Western International University

Arkansas
Arkansas State University
Arkansas State University–Beebe
Arkansas Tech University
Cossatot Technical College
Garland County Community College
Henderson State University
John Brown University
Mississippi County Community College
Ozarka College
Phillips Community College of the University of Arkansas
Pulaski Technical College
Southern Arkansas University
University of Arkansas at Little Rock
University of Arkansas at Monticello
University of Arkansas at Pine Bluff
University of Arkansas Community College at Hope
University of Central Arkansas
Westark College

California
Allan Hancock College
American River College
Armstrong University
Azusa Pacific University
Bakersfield College
Barstow College
Butte-Glenn Community College District
California Baptist University
California College for Health Sciences
California Maritime Academy
California National University for Advanced Studies

California Paramedical and Technical College
California Polytechnic State University–San Luis Obispo
California State Polytechnic University–Pomona
California State University–Bakersfield
California State University–Dominguez Hills
California State University–Fresno
California State University–Fullerton
California State University–Hayward
California State University–Long Beach
California State University–Los Angeles
California State University–Northridge
California State University–Sacramento
California State University–San Marcos
California State University–Stanislaus
Cerritos College
Cerro Coso Community College
Chaffey College
Chapman University
Citrus College
Coastline Community College
Cogswell Polytechnical College
College of the Canyons
College of the Sequoias
Concordia University
Copper Mountain College
Cosumnes River College
Crafton Hills College
Cypress College
De Anza College
Diablo Valley College
Fashion Institute of Design and Merchandising
Fielding Institute
Foothill College
Foundation College
Fresno City College
Gavilan College
Golden Gate University
Golden West College
Hartnell College
Heald College–School of Business and Technology at Hayward

Holy Names College
Irvine Valley College
John F. Kennedy University
Los Angeles City College
Los Angeles Pierce College
Los Angeles Trade–Technical College
Masters Institute
Merced College
Miracosta College
Monterey Institute of International Studies
Monterey Peninsula College
Moorpark College
Mount Saint Mary's College
National University
Newschool of Architecture
Orange Coast College
Pacific Graduate School of Psychology
Palomar College
Patten College
Riverside Community College District
San Diego City College
San Diego Miramar College
San Diego State University
San Francisco State University
San Joaquin Delta College
Santa Monica College
Scripps College
Simpson College
Solano Community College
Southern California Institute of Technology
Southwestern College
Taft College
Touro University International
United States International University
University of La Verne
University of Sarasota–California Campus
University of West Los Angeles
Victor Valley College
West Hills College
Yuba Community College

Colorado
Aims Community College
Arapahoe Community College
Colorado Northwestern Community College
Colorado School of Mines
Colorado State University
Colorado Technical University
Community College of Aurora
Community College of Denver
Denver Automotive and Diesel College
Front Range Community College
Jones International University
Lamar Community College
Mesa State College
Metropolitan State College of Denver
Morgan Community College
Northeastern Junior College
Otero Junior College
Pikes Peak Community College
Pueblo Community College
Red Rocks Community College
Regis University
Trinidad State Junior College
University of Colorado–Colorado Springs
University of Northern Colorado–Center for Professional Development
    and Outreach
University of Southern Colorado–Division of Continuing Education
Western State College
Westwood College of Aviation Technology
Westwood College of Technology

Connecticut
Albertus Magnus College
Asnuntuck Community College
Briarwood College
Capital Community–Technical College
Charter Oak State College
Eastern Connecticut State University
Middlesex Community–Technical College
Mitchell College

Naugatuck Valley Community College
Norwalk Community College
Quinebaug Valley Community College
Sacred Heart University
Southern Connecticut State University
Teikyo Post University
Three Rivers Community College, Mohegan Campus
Tunxis Community College
University of New Haven
Western Connecticut State University

Delaware
Delaware Technical and Community College
Goldey-Beacom College
Wesley College
Wilmington College

District of Columbia
Catholic University of America–Metropolitan College
George Washington University
Howard University
Potomac College
Southeastern University
Strayer University
University of the District of Columbia

Florida
American College of Prehospital Medicine
Atlantic Coast Institute
Barry University–School of Adult and Continuing Education
Bethune-Cookman College
Brevard Community College
Broward Community College
Central Florida Community College
Daytona Beach Community College
Eckerd College–Program for Experienced Learners
Edison Community College
Embry-Riddle Aeronautical University
Everglades College
Florida Agricultural and Mechanical University

Florida Community College at Jacksonville
Florida Gulf Coast University
Florida Institute of Technology
Florida International University
Florida Keys Community College
Florida National College
Florida State University
Florida State University–Panama Canal Branch
Gulf Coast Community College
Hillsborough Community College
Indian River Community College
Jacksonville University
Kaplan College
Keiser College
Lake City Community College
Lake-Sumter Community College
Manatee Community College
Miami-Dade Community College
North Florida Community College
Nova Southeastern University
Okaloosa-Walton Community College
Palm Beach Community College
Pasco-Hernando Community College
Pensacola Junior College
Polk Community College
Rollins College–Brevard Campus
Saint Leo University
Saint Petersburg Junior College
Santa Fe Community College
Seminole Community College
South Florida Community College
Southeastern College
University of Central Florida
University of Florida
University of North Florida
University of South Florida
University of Tampa
University of West Florida
Valencia Community College
Webber College

Georgia
Abraham Baldwin Agricultural College
Albany State University
Albany Technical College
Altamaha Technical College
American InterContinental University
Armstrong Atlantic State University
Athens Technical College
Atlanta Technical College
Augusta Technical College
Brenau University–Evening and Weekend College
Central Georgia Technical College
Chattahoochee Technical College
Clayton College and State University
Coastal Georgia Community College
Columbus State University
Columbus Technical College
Covenant College
Darton College
DeKalb Technical College
East Central Technical Institute
East Georgia College
Emmanuel College
Georgia College and State University
Georgia Military College
Georgia Perimeter College
Georgia Southern University
Georgia Southwestern State University
Gwinnett Technical College
Lanier Technical Institute
Life University–School of Arts and Sciences
Middle Georgia College
Middle Georgia Technical College
Morris Brown College
North Georgia College and State University
North Georgia Technical Institute
North Metro Technical College
Northwestern Technical College
Paine College
Savannah State University

Savannah Technical College
Shorter College–School of Professional Programs
South College
South Georgia College
Southeastern Technical College
Southern Polytechnic State University
Southwest Georgia Technical College
State University of West Georgia
Swainsboro Technical College
Valdosta State University
West Central Technical College
West Georgia Technical College

Guam
Guam Community College
University of Guam

Hawaii
Chaminade University of Honolulu
Hawaii Pacific University
Honolulu Community College
Kapiolani Community College
Leeward Community College
University of Hawaii at Manoa–Outreach College
Windward Community College

Idaho
Boise State University
College of Southern Idaho
Gem State College
Idaho State University
Lewis-Clark State College
North Idaho College
Northwest Nazarene University
Ricks College
University of Idaho

Illinois
Barat College
Benedictine University

Black Hawk College
Carl Sandburg College
City Colleges of Chicago Harold Washington College
College of Lake County
Columbia College Chicago
DeVry Institutes of Technology
Eastern Illinois University
Finch University of Health Sciences, The Chicago Medical School
Governors State University
Highland Community College
Illinois Central College
Illinois Eastern Community Colleges–Frontier, Lincoln Trail, Olney
    Central, and Wabash Valley
Illinois State University
Illinois Valley Community College
John A. Logan College
John Wood Community College
Joliet Junior College
Kaskaskia College
Kendall College
Kishwaukee College
Lake Land College
Lewis and Clark Community College
Lewis University
Lincoln Land Community College
MacMurray College
McKendree College
Midstate College
Morrison Institute of Technology
National-Louis University
Northeastern Illinois University
Olivet Nazarene University
Parkland College
Prairie State College
Quincy University
Rend Lake College
Robert Morris College
Saint Xavier University
Sauk Valley Community College
Shawnee Community College

South Suburban College
Southeastern Illinois College
Southern Illinois University at Edwardsville
Southern Illinois University Carbondale–College of Applied Sciences and Arts
Southern Illinois University Carbondale–College of Education
Southern Illinois University Carbondale–College of Engineering
Southwestern Illinois College
Spoon River College
Trinity Christian College
Triton College
University of Saint Francis
Waubonsee Community College
Western Illinois University–School of Extended and Continuing Education
William Rainey Harper College

Indiana
Ball State University
Bethel College
Calumet College of Saint Joseph
Huntington College
Indiana Institute of Technology
Indiana State University
Indiana University
Indiana University–Purdue University Fort Wayne
Indiana University–Purdue University Indianapolis
Indiana University South Bend–School of Continuing Studies
Indiana Wesleyan University
ITT Technical Institutes
Ivy Tech State College–Central Indiana
Ivy Tech State College–Columbus
Ivy Tech State College–Kokomo/Logansport
Ivy Tech State College–Lafayette
Ivy Tech State College–Northcentral
Ivy Tech State College–Northeast
Ivy Tech State College–Northwest
Ivy Tech State College–Southcentral
Ivy Tech State College–Southeast
Ivy Tech State College–Southwest

Ivy Tech State College–Wabash Valley
Ivy Tech State College–Whitewater
Lincoln Technical Institute
Marian College
Martin University
Oakland City University
Saint Joseph's College
Tri-State University
University of Evansville–External Studies Program
University of Indianapolis
University of Saint Francis
University of Southern Indiana
Vincennes University

Iowa
Briar Cliff College
Central College
Clarke College
Des Moines Area Community College
Drake University
Eastern Iowa Community College District
Ellsworth Community College
Graceland University
Grand View College
Hamilton College
Hawkeye Community College
Indian Hills Community College
Iowa Central Community College
Iowa Lakes Community College
Iowa State University
Iowa Wesleyan College
Iowa Western Community College
Kirkwood Community College
Loras College
Maharishi University of Management
Marshalltown Community College
Marycrest International University
Mount Saint Clare College
North Iowa Area Community College
Northeast Iowa Community College

Northwest Iowa Community College
Palmer College of Chiropractic
Quest College
Saint Ambrose University
Scott Community College
Southwestern Community College
University of Dubuque
University of Iowa
University of Northern Iowa
Upper Iowa University
William Penn University

Kansas
Allen County Community College
Baker University–School of Professional and Graduate Studies
Barton County Community College
Butler County Community College
Cloud County Community College
Coffeyville Community College
Colby Community College
Cowley County Community College
Dodge City Community College
Donnelly College
Emporia State University
Fort Hays State University
Fort Scott Community College
Garden City Community College
Hutchinson Community College and Area Vocational School
Independence Community College
Johnson County Community College
Kansas City Kansas Community College
Kansas State University
Kansas Wesleyan University
Neosho County Community College
Newman University
Ottawa University
Pittsburg State University
Pratt Community College
Saint Mary College
Seward County Community College

University of Kansas
Washburn University
Wichita State University

Kentucky
Ashland Community College
Bellarmine College
Brescia University
Eastern Kentucky University
Elizabethtown Community College
Fugazzi College
Hazard Community College
Henderson Community College
Hopkinsville Community College
Kentucky State University
Kentucky Wesleyan College
Lees College Campus of Hazard Community College
Lindsey Wilson College
Madisonville Community College
Maysville Community College
Morehead State University
Murray State University
National College of Business and Technology
Owensboro Community College
Paducah Community College
Pikeville College
Prestonsburg Community College
Somerset Community College
Sullivan University
Thomas More College
Union College
University of Louisville
West Kentucky Technical College
Western Kentucky University

Louisiana
Education America–Remington College
Grambling State University
Grantham College of Engineering
Louisiana State University and Agricultural and Mechanical College

Louisiana State University at Alexandria
Louisiana State University at Eunice
Louisiana Tech University
Louisiana Technical College Morgan Smith Campus
Louisiana Technical College Northeast Campus
Louisiana Technical College System
Louisiana Technical College Young Memorial Campus
Loyola University New Orleans
McNeese State University
Northwestern State University
Our Lady of Holy Cross College
Southeastern Louisiana University
Southern University at New Orleans
University of Louisiana at Lafayette
University of Louisiana at Monroe
University of New Orleans

Maine
Central Maine Technical College
Eastern Maine Technical College
Kennebec Valley Technical College
Maine College of Art
Maine Maritime Academy
Northern Maine Technical College
Saint Joseph's College of Maine
Thomas College
University of Maine
University of Maine at Augusta
University of Maine at Farmington
University of Maine at Fort Kent
University of Maine at Machias
University of Maine at Presque Isle
University of Southern Maine
Washington County Technical College
York County Technical College

Maryland
Allegany College of Maryland
Anne Arundel Community College
Baltimore City Community College

Bowie State University
Capitol College
Carroll Community College
Cecil Community College
Chesapeake College
College of Southern Maryland
Columbia Union College
Community College of Baltimore County–Catonsville Campus
Community College of Baltimore County–Dundalk Campus
Community College of Baltimore County–Essex Campus
Coppin State College
Frederick Community College
Frostburg State University
Garrett Community College
Hagerstown Community College
Harford Community College
Howard Community College
Montgomery College
Morgan State University
Mount Saint Mary's College–Weekend College
Prince George's Community College
Saint Mary's College of Maryland
Salisbury State University
Towson University
University of Baltimore
University of Maryland–Eastern Shore
University of Maryland–University College
Villa Julie College

Massachusetts
American International College
Anna Maria College
Bay Path College
Becker College
Berkshire Community College
Boston University–Metropolitan College
Bridgewater State College
Bristol Community College
Bunker Hill Community College
Cape Cod Community College

Eastern Nazarene College–LEAD Program
Elms College
Fisher College
Fitchburg State College
Greenfield Community College
Massasoit Community College
Middlesex Community College
Mount Wachusett Community College
Newbury College
Nichols College
North Shore Community College
Northeastern University–University College
Northern Essex Community College
Quincy College
Quinsigamond Community College
Salem State College
Stonehill College–Undergraduate and Continuing Education Programs
Suffolk University
University of Massachusetts Amherst
University of Massachusetts Dartmouth
University of Massachusetts Lowell
Western New England College

Michigan
Baker College
Central Michigan University–College of Extended Learning
Charles Stewart Mott Community College
Cornerstone University
Davenport University
Davenport University–Central Region
Delta College
Eastern Michigan University
Ferris State University
Glen Oaks Community College
Kalamazoo Valley Community College
Kellogg Community College
Kirtland Community College
Lake Michigan College
Lansing Community College
Madonna University

Mid Michigan Community College
Muskegon Community College
North Central Michigan College
Northern Michigan University
Northwood University
Rochester College–College of Extended Learning
Saint Clair County Community College
Schoolcraft College
Siena Heights University
Southwestern Michigan College
Spring Arbor College
University of Michigan–Flint
Washtenaw Community College
Wayne County Community College
Western Michigan University

Minnesota
Alexandria Technical College
Anoka-Ramsey Community College
Augsburg College
Bemidji State University
Bethel College–Center for Graduate and Continuing Studies
Capella University
Central Lakes College
Century College
College of Saint Scholastica
Concordia University, Saint Paul
Lake Superior College
Mesabi Range Community and Technical College
Metropolitan State University
Minnesota State University, Mankato
Minnesota West Community and Technical College–Worthington
    Campus
Normandale Community College
North Hennepin Community College
Northland Community and Technical College
Northwest Technical College
Northwestern College
Pine Technical College
Rainy River Community College

Rasmussen College–St. Cloud
Ridgewater College
Riverland Community College
Saint Cloud State University
Saint Cloud Technical College
Saint Paul Technical College
Southwest State University
Vermilion Community College
Walden University

Mississippi
Alcorn State University
Belhaven College
Coahoma Community College
Copiah-Lincoln Community College
Delta State University
East Central Community College
East Mississippi Community College
Hinds Community College
Holmes Community College
Itawamba Community College
Jackson State University
Jones County Junior College
Mary Holmes College
Meridian Community College
Mississippi Gulf Coast Community College
Mississippi State University
Mississippi University for Women
Mississippi Valley State University
Northwest Mississippi Community College
Pearl River Community College
Rust College
Southwest Mississippi Community College
University of Mississippi
University of Southern Mississippi
William Carey College

Missouri
Central Missouri State University
Columbia College
Culver-Stockton College
Drury University, Mid-Missouri Region (Fort Leonard Wood)
East Central College
Fontbonne College
Global University
Hannibal-LaGrange College
Jefferson College
Lincoln University
Lindenwood University
Maryville University of Saint Louis
Metropolitan Community Colleges
Mineral Area College
Missouri Southern State College
Missouri Valley College
Missouri Western State College
Moberly Area Community College
North Central Missouri College
Northwest Missouri State University
Ozarks Technical Community College
Park University
Rockhurst University
Saint Charles County Community College
Saint Louis University–School for Professional Studies
Sanford-Brown College
Southeast Missouri State University
Southwest Baptist University
Southwest Missouri State University–Springfield
Southwest Missouri State University–West Plains
State Fair Community College
Stephens College–School of Graduate and Continuing Education
University of Missouri–Columbia
University of Missouri–Rolla
University of Missouri–Saint Louis
Webster University
Westminster College
William Jewell College
William Woods University–College of Graduate and Adult Studies

Montana
Blackfeet Community College
Carroll College
Dawson Community College
Flathead Valley Community College
Fort Belknap College
Fort Peck Community College
Helena College of Technology of the University of Montana
Miles Community College
Montana State University–Billings
Montana State University–Bozeman
Montana State University–Great Falls College of Technology
Montana State University–Northern
Montana Tech College of Technology
Montana Tech of the University of Montana
Rocky Mountain College
Salish Kootenai College
Stone Child College
University of Great Falls
University of Montana
University of Montana–Missoula College of Technology
Western Montana College

Nebraska
Bellevue University
Central Community College–Columbus Campus
Central Community College–Grand Island Campus
Central Community College–Hastings Campus
Chadron State College
Clarkson College
Dana College
Hastings College
Metropolitan Community College
Mid-Plains Community College
Nebraska Methodist College of Nursing and Allied Health
Northeast Community College
Peru State College
Southeast Community College
University of Nebraska–Lincoln
University of Nebraska at Kearney

University of Nebraska at Omaha–College of Continuing Studies
Wayne State College
Western Nebraska Community College

Nevada
Career College of Northern Nevada
Community College of Southern Nevada
Great Basin College
Truckee Meadows Community College
University of Nevada, Reno
University of Nevada–Las Vegas
Western Nevada Community College

New Hampshire
Colby-Sawyer College
College for Lifelong Learning
Daniel Webster College
McIntosh College
New England College
New Hampshire College
New Hampshire Community Technical College at Laconia
New Hampshire Community Technical College at Manchester
New Hampshire Community Technical College at Stratham
Rivier College–School of Undergraduate Studies
Undergraduate Evening School
White Pines College

New Jersey
Atlantic Cape Community College
Bergen Community College
Berkeley College
Bloomfield College
Brookdale Community College
Burlington County College
Caldwell College
Camden County College
Centenary College
County College of Morris
Fairleigh Dickinson University
Georgian Court College

Gloucester County College
Kean University
Mercer County Community College
Monmouth University
New Jersey Institute of Technology
Ocean County College
Ramapo College of New Jersey
Raritan Valley Community College
Rider University–College of Continuing Studies
Saint Peter's College
Salem Community College
Sussex County Community College
Thomas Edison State College
Union County College

New Mexico
Clovis Community College
College of Santa Fe
College of the Southwest
Eastern New Mexico University–Main Campus
Eastern New Mexico University–Roswell
Mesa Technical College
New Mexico Highlands University
New Mexico Military Institute
New Mexico State University Dona Ana Branch
Northern New Mexico Community College
San Juan College
Santa Fe Community College
Western New Mexico University

New York
Adelphi University–University College
Adirondack Community College
Berkeley College of New York City
Briarcliffe College
Broome Community College
Canisius College
Cayuga Community College
City University of New York–College of Staten Island
City University of New York–John Jay College of Criminal Justice

City University of New York–Medgar Evers College
Clinton Community College
College of Aeronautics
College of Mount Saint Vincent
College of Saint Rose
Columbia-Greene Community College
Corning Community College
D'Youville College
Daemen College
Dominican College of Blauvelt
Dutchess Community College
Elmira College
Erie Community College
Excelsior College
Genesee Community College
Herkimer County Community College
Hilbert College
Houghton College
Hudson Valley Community College
Iona College
Jamestown Community College
Jefferson Community College
Keuka College
Laboratory Institute of Merchandising
Long Island University–Brooklyn Campus
Long Island University–C.W. Post Campus
Long Island University–Southampton College
Medaille College
Mercy College
Mohawk Valley Community College
Monroe Community College
Mount Saint Mary College
Nassau Community College
Nazareth College of Rochester
New York Institute of Technology
Niagara County Community College
Niagara University
North Country Community College
Nyack College
Orange County Community College

Pace University
Plaza Business Institute
Purchase College, State University of New York
Roberts Wesleyan College
Rochester Institute of Technology
Rockland Community College
Saint Bonaventure University
Saint Francis College
Saint John Fisher College
Saint Joseph's College
Saint Thomas Aquinas College
Schenectady County Community College
Skidmore College–University Without Walls
State University of New York at Binghamton
State University of New York at Buffalo
State University of New York at Farmingdale
State University of New York–College at Brockport
State University of New York–College at Buffalo
State University of New York–College at Fredonia
State University of New York–College at Oswego
State University of New York–College at Plattsburgh
State University of New York–College at Potsdam
State University of New York–College of Agriculture and Technology at Cobleskill
State University of New York–College of Agriculture and Technology at Morrisville
State University of New York–College of Technology at Alfred
State University of New York–College of Technology at Canton
State University of New York–College of Technology at Delhi
State University of New York–Empire State College
State University of New York–Institute of Technology at Utica-Rome
State University of New York–Maritime College
Suffolk County Community College
Sullivan County Community College
Syracuse University–University College
Tompkins Cortland Community College
Touro College
Ulster County Community College
Utica School of Commerce
Villa Maria College of Buffalo

North Carolina
Beaufort County Community College
Belmont Abbey College
Bladen Community College
Caldwell Community College and Technical Institute
Campbell University
Cape Fear Community College
Catawba Valley Community College
Central Carolina Community College
Central Piedmont Community College
Cleveland Community College
Coastal Carolina Community College
College of the Albemarle
Craven Community College
Davidson County Community College
Durham Technical Community College
East Carolina University
Edgecombe Community College
Elizabeth City State University
Fayetteville State University
Fayetteville Technical Community College
Guilford Technical Community College
Halifax Community College
Haywood Community College
High Point University
Isothermal Community College
Johnson C. Smith University
Johnston Community College
Lenoir Community College
Mars Hill College
Martin Community College
Mayland Community College
Methodist College
Mitchell Community College
Montgomery Community College
Montreat College
Mount Olive College
Nash Community College
North Carolina A&T University
North Carolina Central University

North Carolina State University
North Carolina Wesleyan College
Pfeiffer University
Piedmont Community College
Pitt Community College
Randolph Community College
Richmond Community College
Roanoke-Chowan Community College
Rockingham Community College
Rowan-Cabarrus Community College
Sandhills Community College
South Piedmont Community College
Stanly Community College
Surry Community College
University of North Carolina at Charlotte
University of North Carolina at Pembroke
University of North Carolina at Wilmington
Wake Technical Community College
Wayne Community College
Western Carolina University
Western Piedmont Community College
Wilkes Community College
Wingate University

North Dakota
Bismarck State College
Dickinson State University
Jamestown College
Mayville State University
Minot State University
North Dakota State College of Science
North Dakota State University
University of Mary
University of North Dakota–Lake Region
University of North Dakota–Main Campus
Valley City State University

Ohio
Ashland University
Bowling Green State University

Capital University
Central State University
Cincinnati State Technical and Community College
Circleville Bible College
Clark State Community College
Cleveland Institute of Electronics
Cleveland State University
Columbus State Community College
Cuyahoga Community College
Davis College
Defiance College
Edison State Community College
Franklin University
Hocking College
Kent State University
Lakeland Community College
Lima Technical College
Lorain County Community College
Lourdes College
Malone College
Mercy College of Northwest Ohio
Miami-Jacobs College
North Central Technical College
Northwest State Community College
Ohio Dominican College
Ohio Northern University
Ohio State University
Ohio State University–Lima Campus
Ohio University
Otterbein College
Shawnee State University
Sinclair Community College
Southern State Community College
Tiffin University
Union Institute
University of Akron
University of Akron–Wayne College
University of Cincinnati–College of Evening and Continuing
     Education
University of Cincinnati–Raymond Walters College

University of Findlay
University of Northwestern Ohio
University of Rio Grande
University of Toledo
Urbana University
Washington State Community College
Wilberforce University
Wright State University
Xavier University
Youngstown State University

Oklahoma
Bacone College
Cameron University
Carl Albert State College
Connors State College
East Central University
Eastern Oklahoma State College
Langston University
Murray State College
Northeastern Oklahoma A&M College
Northeastern State University
Northern Oklahoma College
Northwestern Oklahoma State University
Oklahoma City Community College
Oklahoma City University
Oklahoma State University–Main Campus
Oklahoma State University–Oklahoma City
Oklahoma State University–Okmulgee
Oral Roberts University
Redlands Community College
Rogers State University
Rose State College
Saint Gregory's University
Southeastern Oklahoma State University
Southwestern Oklahoma State University
Tulsa Community College
University of Central Oklahoma
University of Oklahoma

University of Oklahoma–College of Continuing Education and
Advanced Programs and College of Liberal Studies
University of Science and Arts of Oklahoma
University of Tulsa
Western Oklahoma State College

Oregon
Art Institute of Portland
Blue Mountain Community College
Clackamas Community College
Concordia University
Eastern Oregon University
Eugene Bible College
George Fox University
Lane Community College
Marylhurst University
Mount Hood Community College
Northwest Christian College
Oregon Health Sciences University
Oregon Institute of Technology
Oregon State University
Portland Community College
Rogue Community College
Southern Oregon University
Southwestern Oregon Community College
Treasure Valley Community College
Umpqua Community College
University of Oregon
Warner Pacific College
Western Baptist College
Western Oregon University

Pennsylvania
Art Institute of Pittsburgh
Beaver College
Bloomsburg University of Pennsylvania
Bucks County Community College
Butler County Community College
Cabrini College

California University of Pennsylvania
Cambria-Rowe Business College
Carlow College
Cedar Crest College–Continuing Education Programs
Clarion University of Pennsylvania
Community College of Allegheny County
Delaware Valley College
DeSales University
Drexel University
East Stroudsburg University
Eastern College
Edinboro University of Pennsylvania
Education American–Vale Technical Institute
Gwynedd-Mercy College
Harcourt Learning Direct Center for Degree Studies
Harcum College
Harrisburg Area Community College
Holy Family College
Indiana University of Pennsylvania
Johnson Technical Institute
Keystone College
King's College
La Roche College
La Salle University
Lackawanna Junior College
Lancaster Bible College
Lebanon Valley College
Lehigh Carbon Community College
Lincoln Technical Institute, Allentown
Lincoln Technical Institute, Philadelphia
Lock Haven University of Pennsylvania
Luzerne County Community College
Mansfield University of Pennsylvania
Marywood University
Millersville University of Pennsylvania
Montgomery County Community College
Mount Aloysius College
Neumann College
Northampton Community College
Peirce College

Penn State Harrisburg–Capital College
Penn State World Campus
Pennsylvania College of Technology
Pennsylvania Institute of Technology
Point Park College
Robert Morris College
Saint Francis College
Saint Vincent College
Seton Hall College
Slippery Rock University of Pennsylvania
Temple University
Thompson Institute
University of Scranton–Dexter Hanley College
Valley Forge Military College
Waynesburg College
Westmoreland County Community College
Widener University
Wilson College–College of Continuing Education Division Continuing
   Studies
York College of Pennsylvania

Puerto Rico
American University of Puerto Rico
Caribbean University
Electronic Data Processing College of Puerto Rico
Inter American University of Puerto Rico Universidad Metropolitana
University of Puerto Rico–Humacao University College

Rhode Island
Community College of Rhode Island
Johnson and Wales University
Providence College–School of Continuing Education
Rhode Island College
Roger Williams University–University College
Salve Regina University
University of Rhode Island–Feinstein College of Continuing Education

South Carolina
Aiken Technical College
Benedict College

Central Carolina Technical College
Charleston Southern University
Claflin College
Coastal Carolina University
Coker College
Denmark Technical College
Florence-Darlington Technical College
Francis Marion University
Greenville Technical College
Horry-Georgetown Technical College
Johnson and Wales University at Charleston
Lander University
Limestone College
Midlands Technical College
Newberry College
North Greenville College
Northeastern Technical College
Orangeburg-Calhoun Technical College
Piedmont Technical College
Southern Wesleyan University
Spartanburg Methodist College
Spartanburg Technical College
Technical College of the Lowcountry
Trident Technical College
University of South Carolina–Aiken
University of South Carolina–Beaufort
University of South Carolina–Columbia
University of South Carolina–Sumter
University of South Carolina–Spartanburg
Williamsburg Technical College
Wofford College

South Dakota
Augustana College
Black Hills State University
Dakota State University
Dakota Wesleyan University
Huron University–A Campus of Colorado Technical University
Kilian Community College
Mitchell Technical Institute

Mount Marty College
National American University
Northern State University
South Dakota School of Mines and Technology
South Dakota State University
University of South Dakota
Western Dakota Technical Institute

Tennessee
Aquinas College
Austin Peay State University–Fort Campbell Campus
Bethel College
Bryan College–Adult Degree Completion Programs (ASPIRE)
Carson-Newman College
Chattanooga State Technical Community College
Cleveland State Community College
Crichton College
Cumberland University
Dyersburg State Community College
East Tennessee State University
Hiwassee College
Jackson State Community College
King College
Lambuth University
Lane College
LeMoyne-Owen College
Lincoln Memorial University
Martin Methodist College
Middle Tennessee State University
Milligan College
Motlow State Community College
Nashville State Technical Institute
North Central Institute
Northeast State Technical Community College
Pellissippi State Technical Community College
Roane State Community College
Southern Adventist University
Southwest Tennessee Community College
Tennessee State University
Tennessee Technological University

Tennessee Wesleyan College
Tusculum College
Union University
University of Tennessee at Chattanooga
University of Tennessee at Martin
University of Tennessee–Health Science Center
University of Tennessee, Knoxville
Walters State Community College

Texas
Abilene Christian University
Angelina College
Angelo State University
Austin Community College
Central Texas College
Clarendon College
College of the Mainland
Collin County Community College
Concordia University at Austin
Dallas Baptist University
Dallas County Community College District
Dallas County Community College District–Richland College
Del Mar College
El Centro College
El Paso County Community College District
ESS College of Business
Frank Phillips College
Galveston College
Grayson County College
Hardin-Simmons University
Houston Community College System
Howard Payne University
Jarvis Christian College
Kilgore College
Lamar University
Laredo Community College
Lee College
Lubbock Christian University
McMurry University
Midland College

Midwestern State University
Navarro College
North Central Texas College
North Harris Montgomery Community College District
North Lake College
Odessa College
Our Lady of the Lake University
Palo Alto College
Paris Junior College
Prairie View A&M University
Ranger College
Saint Mary's University
Saint Philip's College
Sam Houston State University
San Antonio College
Schreiner College
South Plains College
Southwest Texas Junior College
Southwest Texas State University–Occupational Education Program
Southwestern Adventist University
Sul Ross State University
Tarleton State University
Temple College
Texarkana College
Texas A&M University–Commerce
Texas A&M University–Corpus Christi
Texas A&M University–Kingsville
Texas Lutheran University
Texas State Technical College–Harlingen
Texas State Technical College–Sweetwater
Texas State Technical College at Waco
Texas Tech University
Texas Woman's University
Trinity Valley Community College
Tyler Junior College
Universal Technical Institute
University of Dallas–Constantin College
University of Houston–Clear Lake
University of Houston–Conrad N. Hilton College of Hotel and
    Restaurant Management

University of Mary Hardin–Baylor
University of North Texas
University of Saint Thomas
University of Texas–Pan American
University of Texas at Arlington
University of Texas at Brownsville
University of Texas at El Paso
University of Texas at San Antonio
University of Texas of the Permian Basin
University of the Incarnate Word
Vernon Regional Junior College
Wade College
Wayland Baptist University
Weatherford College
West Texas A&M University
Western Texas College
Wiley College

Utah
Certified Careers Institute
College of Eastern Utah
Dixie College
Mountain West College
Salt Lake Community College
Snow College
Southern Utah University
Utah State University
Utah Valley State College
Weber State University
Westminster College of Salt Lake City

Vermont
Champlain College
Community College of Vermont
Norwich University–Vermont College
Southern Vermont College
University of Vermont
Vermont Technical College

Virgin Islands
University of the Virgin Islands

Virginia
American Military University
Averett College
Blue Ridge Community College
Bryant and Stratton College
Central Virginia Community College
Christopher Newport University
Dabney S. Lancaster Community College
ECPI College of Technology
George Mason University–Bachelor of Individualized Study Program
Germanna Community College
Hampton University
J. Sargeant Reynolds Community College
James Madison University
John Tyler Community College
Liberty University–External Degree Program
Lord Fairfax Community College
Marymount University
National Business College
New River Community College
Norfolk State University
Northern Virginia Community College
Old Dominion University
Paul D. Camp Community College
Piedmont Virginia Community College
Rappahannock Community College
Richard Bland College
Saint Paul's College
Shenandoah University
Southside Virginia Community College
Southwest Virginia Community College
Thomas Nelson Community College
Tidewater Community College
University of Virginia's College at Wise
Virginia Intermont College

Virginia State University
Virginia Western Community College
World College
Wytheville Community College

Washington
Big Bend Community College
Central Washington University
City University
Community Colleges of Spokane
Eastern Washington University
Edmonds Community College
Everett Community College
Grays Harbor College
Green River Community College
Heritage College
Highline Community College
Lower Columbia College
Olympic College
Pacific Lutheran University
Peninsula College
Pierce College
Renton Technical College
Saint Martin's College
Seattle Central Community College
Skagit Valley College–Whidbey Campus
South Puget Sound Community College
Tacoma Community College
Trinity Lutheran College
University of Washington
Walla Walla Community College
Washington State University
Wenatchee Valley College
Whatcom Community College
Yakima Valley Community College

West Virginia
Bethany College
Bluefield State College
Concord College–Board of Regents Program

Davis and Elkins College
Fairmont State College
Glenville State College
Marshall University
Mountain State University
Ohio Valley College
Salem International University
Shepherd College
Southern West Virginia Community and Technical College
University of Charleston
West Liberty State College
West Virginia Junior College at Morgantown
West Virginia State College
West Virginia University
West Virginia University Institute of Technology
West Virginia Wesleyan College
Wheeling Jesuit University

Wisconsin
Bryant and Stratton College
Cardinal Stritch College
Carroll College
Chippewa Valley Technical College
Concordia University
Gateway Technical College
Herzing College–Madison
Lakeland College–William R. Kellett School of Lifelong Learning
Lakeshore Technical College
Milwaukee Area Technical College
Milwaukee School of Engineering
Mount Mary College
Mount Senario College
Silver Lake College
Southwest Wisconsin Technical College
University of Wisconsin–Eau Claire
University of Wisconsin–La Crosse
University of Wisconsin–Oshkosh
University of Wisconsin–Parkside
University of Wisconsin–Platteville
University of Wisconsin–Stevens Point

University of Wisconsin–Stout
University of Wisconsin–Superior
University of Wisconsin–Whitewater
University of Wisconsin Colleges
Viterbo University
Western Wisconsin Technical College
Wisconsin Indianhead Technical College

Wyoming
Casper College
Central Wyoming College
Eastern Wyoming College
Laramie County Community College
Northern Wyoming Community College District–Sheridan College,
    Gillette Campus
Northwest College
University of Wyoming
Western Wyoming Community College

16

College via the Internet

Anyone who uses one of the popular online computer services is probably aware that many colleges and universities offer courses over the Internet. Many schools now offer entire degree programs that can be completed online. The convenience and easy access of these degree programs make them attractive to many servicemembers. A few years ago, most of these degree programs were too expensive for most servicemembers. Today, however, their cost is comparable to the cost of many on-campus courses and degree programs. These web-based programs can be yet another tool for pursuing a degree by nontraditional means.

On the following pages you will find profiles of twelve colleges and universities that offer accredited degrees over the Internet. Most of these schools are well known, and all of them are accredited by either regional accrediting associations or the Distance Education and Training Council (DETC), all of which are recognized by the U.S. Department of Education. Most of these schools also are members of the SOC program, but affiliation with a particular military program was not a prerequisite for the schools profiled on the following pages. Instead, these schools were chosen because they offer nontraditional programs to everyone and represent a sampling of the many Internet-based college programs available to all students. These programs also show that nontraditional forms of education are now part of many mainstream collegiate curriculums. Nontraditional programs are no longer just a shortcut for military personnel or working adults; they are now used by all college students.

While not all of these Internet-based programs are designed specifically for the military, they all are approved by the Department of Veterans Affairs for educational benefits. The particular rules for accepting military training and courses and college-level examinations for degree requirements at these schools vary, but all accept some amount of military training, CLEPs,

DANTES Examinations, ECEs, GREs, and other forms of nontraditional credit.

AMERICAN MILITARY UNIVERSITY
9104-P Manassas Drive
Manassas Park, VA 20111
Phone: (703) 330-5398
Fax: (703) 330-5109
Web address: *www.amunet.edu*

Degrees Offered:
BA in Intelligence Studies
BA in Military History (American or world)
BA in Military Management
MA in Air Warfare
MA in Civil War Studies
MA in Defense Management
MA in Intelligence Studies
MA in Land Warfare
MA in Naval Warfare
MA in Unconventional Warfare

Convenience: There is no residency requirement; all courses can be completed by distance learning.

Accreditation: American Military University (AMU) is accredited by the DETC and is pursuing additional accreditation by the Southern Association of Colleges and Schools.

Approved for Veteran's Benefits: Yes. Participates in the SOC program.

Note: The convenience of AMU's programs makes them perfect for military personnel or adult students with an interest in military history, intelligence, or modern warfare.

ANDREWS UNIVERSITY
HSI Office
Nethery Hall
Andrews University
Berrien Springs, MI 49104-0070
Phone: (800) 471-6210 or (800) 253-2874
Fax: (616) 471-6900
Web address: *www.andrews.edu/AUHSI*

Degrees Offered:
   AA in General Studies: Personal Ministry
   BA in General Studies: Humanities
   BA in Religion
   BS in General Studies: Cross-Cultural Studies
   BS in General Studies: Human Organization and Behavior
   Convenience: There is no residency requirement for the degrees above; all courses can be completed by distance learning.
   Accreditation: Andrews University is accredited by the North Central Association of Colleges and Schools.
   Approved for Veteran's Benefits: Yes. Does not particpate in the SOC program.
   Note: Andrews University awards degrees through its distance education program, through a cooperative arrangement with Home Study International, but all credits are granted by Andrews University, and students receive an Andrews University diploma upon graduation from the program.

CALIFORNIA COLLEGE FOR HEALTH SCIENCES
   222 West 24th Street
   National City, CA 91950
   Phone: (619) 477-4800
   Fax: (619) 477-4360
   Web address: *www.cchs.edu*

Degrees Offered:
   AS in Allied Health
   AS in Early Childhood Education
   AS in EEG Technology
   AS in Medical Transcription
   AS in Respiratory Technology
   AS in Respiratory Therapy
   BS in Business (with majors in accounting, finance, general business, management, or marketing)
   BS in Health Services (with emphasis in management)
   BS in Health Services (with emphasis in respiratory care)
   Master of Public Health
   MBA (with a concentration in healthcare)
   MS in Health Services (with concentrations in community health or wellness promotion)

MS in Healthcare Administration

Convenience: All courses and degrees can be completed by distance learning at home.

Accreditation: California College for Health Sciences is accredited by the DETC.

Approved for Veteran's Benefits: Yes. Participates in the SOC program.

Note: California College for Health Sciences also has many diploma programs available, such as dental assisting, EKG technology, medical assisting, and pharmacy technology, among others.

COLUMBIA UNION COLLEGE

External Degree Program
7600 Flower Avenue
Takoma Park, MD 20912-7796
Phone: (301) 891-4124
Web address: *www.cuc.edu*

Degrees Offered:

AA in General Studies
AS in General Studies
BA in General Studies
BA in Psychology
BA in Religion
BA in Theology
BS in Business Administration
BS in General Studies
BS in Information Systems
BS in Respiratory Care

Convenience: All four-year programs require completion of a minimum of 60 semester hours of college classroom experience from an accredited school.

Accreditation: Columbia Union College is accredited by the Middle States Association of Colleges and Schools.

Approved for Veteran's Benefits: Yes. Participates in the SOC program.

Note: The last 30 semester hours of all four-year programs must be completed via Columbia Union College courses.

EASTERN OREGON UNIVERSITY
Division of Extended Programs
1410 L Avenue
La Grande, OR 97850
Phone: (541) 962-3614
Web address: *www.eou.edu*

Degrees Offered:
AS in Office Administration
BA and BS in Business and Economics
BA and BS in Economics
BA and BS in Liberal Studies
BA and BS in Philosophy
BA and BS in Politics
BS in Physical Education and Health
Convenience: All requirements for the above degrees can be completed over the Internet.

Accreditation: Eastern Oregon University is accredited by the Northwest Association of Colleges and Schools.

Approved for Veteran's Benefits: Yes. Participates in the SOC program.

Note: Eastern Oregon also offers master's degrees in teacher education, school administration, business administration, and social work and programs in nursing and fire services administration, but these are available only to students living in Oregon.

GLOBAL UNIVERSITY (FORMERLY BEREAN UNIVERSITY)
1211 South Glenstone Avenue
Springfield, MO 65802
Phone: (800) 443-1083
Fax: (417) 862-0863
Web address: *www.globaluniversity.edu*

Degrees Offered:
AA in Bible and Theology
AA in Church Ministries
AA in Ministerial Studies
BA in Bible/Christian Counseling
BA in Bible/Christian Education

BA in Bible/Missions: Evangelism
BA in Bible/Pastoral Ministries
BA in Bible/Theology
MA in Biblical Studies
MA in Christian Counseling
MA in Ministerial Studies (with concentrations in leadership, missions, and education)

Convenience: There is no residency requirement; all degrees and courses can be completed by distance learning.

Accreditation: Global University is accredited by the DETC.

Approved for Veteran's Benefits: Yes. Does not participate in the SOC program.

Note: Global University also offers a Spanish curriculum (curso de estudios en español), whereby students can earn an AA degree utilizing all Spanish courses.

GRANTHAM COLLEGE OF ENGINEERING
34641 Grantham College Road
Slidell, LA 70460
Phone: (888) 423-4242 or (504) 649-4191
Fax: (504) 649-4183
Web address: *www.grantham.edu*

Degrees Offered:
AS in Computer Science
AS in Engineering Technology: Computers
AS in Engineering Technology: Electronics
BS in Computer Science
BS in Engineering Technology: Computers
BS in Engineering Technology: Electronics

Convenience: There is no residency requirement; all degrees and courses can be completed by distance learning.

Accreditation: Grantham College is accredited by the DETC.

Approved for Veteran's Benefits: Yes. Participates in the SOC program.

Note: Hundreds of companies and government agencies have reimbursed their employees for completing degrees with Grantham.

IOWA STATE UNIVERSITY
College of Engineering
104 Marston Hall
Ames, IA 50011-2010
Phone: (515) 294-5933
Web address: *www.eng.iastate.edu*

Degrees offered:

Master of Engineering (with programs in aerospace engineering, agricultural engineering, chemical engineering, civil engineering, engineering mechanics, and systems engineering)

MS in Engineering (with programs in aerospace engineering, agricultural engineering, biomedical engineering, ceramic engineering, chemical engineering, civil engineering, computer engineering, electrical engineering, engineering mechanics, industrial engineering, mechanical engineering, metallurgy, and operations research)

Convenience: All requirements for the above degrees can be completed by distance education.

Accreditation: Iowa State University is accredited by the North Central Association of Colleges and Schools.

Approved for Veteran's Benefits: Yes. Participates in the SOC program.

Note: The MS degrees in computer engineering, electrical engineering, industrial engineering, and mechanical engineering are also available in a nonthesis option.

OHIO UNIVERSITY
Tupper Hall 309
Athens, OH 45701
Phone: (800) 444-2420 or (614) 593-2150
Web address: *www.cats.ohiou.edu*

Degrees Offered:

Associate in Applied Business
Associate in Arts
Associate in Individualized Studies
Associate in Sciences
Bachelor in Individualized Studies

Convenience: There is no residency requirement; all degrees and courses can be completed by distance learning.

Accreditation: Ohio University is regionally accredited by the North Central Association of Schools and Colleges.

Approved for Veteran's Benefits: Yes. Participates in the SOC program.

Note: Ohio University has a program for the incarcerated that assists students in prison with furthering their education through distance learning.

SAINT LEO UNIVERSITY

Office of Admission, P.O. Box 6665
Saint Leo, FL 33574-6665
Phone: (800) 334-5532 or (352) 588-8283
Web address: *www.saintleo.edu*

Degrees Offered:

BA in Accounting
BA in Business Administration (accounting specialization)
BA in Business Administration (computer information systems specialization)
BA in Business Administration (general)
BS in Science in computer information systems

Convenience: All requirements for Saint Leo degrees can be completed from home by distance learning.

Accreditation: Saint Leo University is accredited by the Southern Association of Colleges and Schools.

Approved for Veteran's Benefits: Yes. Participates in the SOC program.

Note: Saint Leo was founded in 1889 and is one of the nation's largest providers of higher education to the military. Saint Leo boasts that it has 8,000 students enrolled at 16 campuses throughout the Southeast. Each degree program provides 60 credits, in the form of 20, eight-week three-credit-hour courses. Students entering the program with at least 60 semester hours can earn their Saint Leo College BA or BS degree in about two years.

STANFORD UNIVERSITY

Stanford Center for Professional Development
Stanford, CA 94305
Phone: (650) 725-3000
Web address: *stanford-online.stanford.edu*

Degree Offered: MS in Electrical Engineering

Convenience: All requirements for the MS in Electrical Engineering degree can be completed from home by distance learning.

Accreditation: Stanford University is accredited by the Western Association of Schools and Colleges.

Approved for Veteran's Benefits: Yes. Does not participate in the SOC program.

Note: Stanford points out that its online program was nationally recognized as the "Most Significant Advancement in Distance Learning for 1997" by the U.S. Distance Learning Association. In addition to this and other School of Engineering programs, Stanford Online offers a selection of courses from the School of Earth Sciences and the School of Medicine.

UNIVERSITY COLLEGE, UNIVERSITY OF DENVER

2211 South Josephine Street
Denver, CO 80208
Phone: (800) 347-2042 or (303) 871-3155
Web address: *www.universitycollege.du.edu*

Degrees Offered:

Master of Environmental Policy and Management (optional concentrations in business environmental management, ecotourism management, environmental health and safety, environmental regulatory compliance, management of hazardous materials, and natural resource management)

Master of Telecommunications (optional concentrations in telecommunications technology, strategic networking policy, regulation and assessment, and computer-telephony integration)

Convenience: All requirements for the above degrees can be completed by distance education.

Accreditation: The University of Denver is accredited by the North Central Association of Colleges and Schools.

Approved for Veteran's Benefits: Yes. Does not participate in the SOC program.

Note: University College also offers a 15-quarter-hour certificate in network analysis and design, a 24-quarter-hour certificate in telecommunications, and several 28-quarter-hour certificate programs in environmental policy.

17

Service Educational Benefits and Programs

In addition to the programs described in the previous chapters, soldiers, sailors, airmen, and marines are entitled to a number of important benefits because of their military service. This chapter covers educational counseling and career planning; the Montgomery GI Bill; financial and other types of assistance, including high school completion services, college admissions tests, and information on becoming a teacher; and unique nontraditional educational opportunities. These are all available through your military education center, which is your education headquarters.

MILITARY EDUCATION CENTERS
The education center, regardless of whether it is an Army, Navy, Air Force, or Marine Corps education center, provides the same valuable programs. Of course, resources vary not only among services, but also among installations. Some services may be available only at the military education center where a servicemember's educational records are maintained. As a general rule, however, education counselors provide the same services to military personnel regardless of service affiliation.

Career Planning Programs and Systems Offered
The education center offers many different types of career planning using many unique programs and systems, such as the DANTES Computer Assisted Guidance Information Systems (CAGIS), the Campbell Interest and Skill Survey (CISS), the Career Assessment Inventory (CAI) Enhanced Version, the Holland Self-Directed Search (SDS), the Kuder Occupational Interest Survey, the Strong Interest Inventory (SSI), and the Myers-Briggs Type Indicator (MBTI).

A Typical Education Center

CAGIS is a collection of DANTES interactive computer-assisted guidance and career planning information systems. CAGIS allows individuals to use personal information to interact with the computer to reach more reasonable decisions regarding educational and vocational choices. Currently, there are two systems being used as part of CAGIS: DISCOVER and the Guidance Information System (GIS). DISCOVER is used to assess interests, abilities, and values and provide information on related occupations and educational opportunities. GIS is used to locate facts about colleges, professional schools, occupations, military careers, and financial aid.

CISS is a modern survey that measures self-interests and skills. It is used to help counselors obtain more complete career assessment information. This survey provides both an interest scale and a confidence scale. The interest scale reflects the individual's degree of attraction for a specified occupational area. The confidence scale is a parallel skill scale that provides an estimate of the individual's confidence in his or her ability to perform various occupational activities. Together, these scales provide more comprehensive and valuable data than interest scores alone. CISS focuses on careers that require some degree of college education and is most appropriate for individuals who are college bound.

CAI helps counselors and servicemembers make career decisions by measuring interests requiring a minimum of postsecondary education, such as community college, technical, or business school training. CAI contains basic interest scales that provide more specific information about a person's interests in twenty-five different career areas, such as electronics and medical service occupations. CAI also has occupational scales that relate to 111 specific careers and indicate the interest areas that the individual has in common with employees successfully employed in those particular fields.

SDS is an interest test program that allows servicemembers to find the occupations that best suit their interests and skills. The format is easy to use, and the test can be taken, scored, and interpreted by the individual without assistance. SDS contains an occupational finder that has over 1,300 occupational possibilities.

The Kuder Occupational Interest Survey is a survey that suggests promising occupations and college majors in rank order, based on an individual's pattern. The occupations range from those requiring professional schooling to those requiring technical training. The Kuder is one of the oldest interest surveys on the market today.

SSI is an inventory that measures a person's interest in careers requiring advanced technical or college training. Basic interest scales provide specific information about a person's interests in twenty-three career fields, such as medical science, law and/or politics, and business management. The occupational scales relate to 111 specific careers and indicate areas of career satisfaction.

MBTI is designed to help individuals understand their strengths and evaluate their differences and similarities. It outlines basic differences in perception and judgment. Perception uses sensing and intuition to evaluate the paths to awareness of things, people, happenings, or ideas. Judgment uses thinking and feeling to evaluate all the ways of coming to conclusions about what has been perceived.

MONTGOMERY GI BILL

The Montgomery GI Bill is a program of education benefits for military personnel. It can be used to pay for the following:

1. Courses at colleges and universities leading to associate, bachelor's, and graduate degrees and accredited independent study. Cooperative training programs are available to individuals not on active duty.
2. Courses leading to a certificate or diploma from business, technical, or vocational schools.
3. Apprenticeship or on-the-job training programs for individuals not on active duty.
4. Correspondence courses, under certain conditions.

5. Flight training. Before beginning training, the veteran must have a private pilot's license and meet the physical requirements for a commercial license. Benefits also may be received for flying hours up to the minimum required by the Federal Aviation Administration for the rating or certification being pursued.
6. Tutorial assistance benefits if the individual is enrolled in school half-time or more. Remedial, deficiency, and refresher training also may be available.

Amount Paid by the Montgomery GI Bill

The amount paid by the Montgomery GI Bill is determined by Congress and specified in Chapter 30, Title 38, United States Code. Congress has raised the amounts many times over the years, and legislation signed in 2002 amended the law and raised the amounts again. Veterans who served on active duty for three years or more or who served two years active duty plus four years in the Selected Reserve or National Guard receive thirty-six monthly payments of $800 during fiscal year 2002, $900 during fiscal year 2003, and $985 during fiscal year 2004. For the latest information on GI Bill benefits and payment information, visit the education section of the Veterans Administration website: *www.va.gov.*

Eligibility for Montgomery GI Bill Benefits

Individuals who entered active duty for the first time after 30 June 1985 and received an honorable discharge are eligible for the Montgomery GI Bill. Active duty includes full-time National Guard duty performed after 29 November 1989. To receive the maximum benefit, participants must serve continuously for three years. Individuals also may qualify for the full benefit by serving two continuous years on active duty, followed by four years of Selected Reserve service (the 2x4 program), beginning within one year of release from active duty.

Participants must meet the requirements for a high school diploma or an equivalency certificate before the first period of active duty ends. Completing 12 credit hours toward a college degree meets this requirement. Individuals who serve at least three years of active duty, even though they were initially obligated to serve less, will be paid the maximum benefit.

For the most part, benefits under the Montgomery GI Bill end ten years from the date of the veteran's last discharge or release from active duty. The Veterans Administration can extend this ten-year period if the veteran was prevented from training during this period because of a disability or because he or she was held by a foreign government or power. The ten-year period can also be extended if an individual reenters active duty for ninety days or more after becoming eligible. Veterans serving periods of active duty of less than ninety days can qualify for extensions under certain circumstances. If the veteran's discharge is upgraded by the military, the ten-year period begins on the date of the upgrade. If eligibility is based on two years of active duty and four years in the Selected Reserve (the 2x4 program), the veteran's eligibility will end ten years from release from active duty or ten years from completion of the four-year Selected Reserve obligation, whichever is later. Time spent on active duty for training in the National Guard and Reserves does not establish eligibility for the Montgomery GI Bill.

Enrollment in the Montgomery GI Bill Program
Servicemembers normally enroll in the Montgomery GI Bill Program upon entry into the military. To participate in the Montgomery GI Bill, servicemembers must have their military pay reduced by $100 a month for the first twelve months of active duty. This servicemember contribution to the program is mandatory, and this money is not refundable. If an individual decides not to participate in this program, this decision cannot be changed at a later date, except in special circumstances. An exception is made for servicemembers who are involuntarily separated from active duty with an honorable discharge. A second exception is made for those who voluntarily separate from active duty under force reduction programs.

OTHER KINDS OF FINANCIAL ASSISTANCE
Financial assistance for college comes in many forms. The experts at the education center can provide valuable information and counseling about all types of financial assistance for college education, including educational grants, scholarships, work-study, and loans. In addition to information about student aid offered by the federal and state governments, the education center maintains information about financial assistance offered by private companies, labor unions, business organizations, foundations, religious organizations, fraternities and sororities, town and city clubs, and community and civic groups, such as the American Legion, YMCA, 4-H Club, Elks, Kiwanis, Jaycees, and Girl or Boy Scouts. The education center also provides the Free Application for Federal Student Aid (FAFSA) form, which is the first step to obtaining student financial aid such as Federal Pell Grants, Federal Stafford Loans, Federal PLUS Loans, Federal Consolidation Loans, Federal Supplemental Educational Opportunity Grants, Federal Work-Study, and Federal Perkins Loans. The latest information on military tuition assistance funding and limitations, including information on the Tuition Assis-

tance Top-up Program, which allows servicemembers to combine a limited amount of their Montgomery GI Bill with tuition assistance, is also available at the education center.

FINISHING HIGH SCHOOL

The education center can help servicemembers receive high school equivalency diplomas through the General Educational Development (GED) test. The GED is designed specifically for those adults who never completed high school. It is composed of a battery of five tests (writing skills, social studies, interpreting literature and the arts, science, and mathematics) designed to measure the general skills and knowledge usually acquired in four years of high school study. These tests were developed by the GED Testing Service according to specifications established by professional educators in each subject area. Servicemembers can earn the equivalent of a high school diploma by passing all five parts of the GED. Each year, hundreds of military personnel earn their high school equivalency by passing the GED.

COLLEGE ADMISSIONS TESTING

The education center administers many different college admissions tests, including the American College Testing (ACT) Assessment Program, the Scholastic Assessment Test (SAT), the Graduate Management Admission Test (GMAT), the Praxis National Teachers Examination (NTE), and the Law School Admission Test (LSAT).

ACT is a program that assesses general educational development and measures the performance of intellectual tasks required by a college student. The examination consists of English, mathematics, reading, and science reasoning.

The SAT measures verbal and mathematical abilities. The verbal portion includes vocabulary, verbal reasoning, and reading comprehension. The mathematical portion tests mathematical reasoning, using arithmetic, algebra, and geometry, and emphasizes problem-solving aptitude rather than advanced achievement in mathematics.

The GMAT measures general verbal and quantitative abilities, developed over a long period of time, that are associated with success in the first year of study at a graduate school of management.

Praxis NTE is actually three separate tests that measure communication skills, general knowledge, and professional knowledge. The Praxis specialty area tests measure understanding of the content and methods applicable to the specific subject area.

The LSAT is designed to assist law schools in assessing the academic potential of their applicants. It measures skills that are considered essential for success in law school, such as the ability to process information to reach conclusions. The LSAT is not funded by DANTES.

HELP IN BECOMING A TEACHER

In addition to many other services, the education center offers information about programs designed to assist servicemembers with their transition into the civilian world. One such program, the Troops to Teachers (TTT) Program, has successfully helped many servicemembers become qualified teachers. The TTT Program is operated by the Department of Education, but DANTES manages the program for the military services. The primary goal of the TTT program is to place math and science teachers, but it places qualified teachers in any subjects taught. The greatest need for teachers is in the rural and inner-city school districts. TTT participants have proved to be strong, positive role models, and they have become especially attractive to the school districts serving a large percentage of students from single-parent families. TTT participants are valued for their strong academic background, leadership skill, personal confidence, maturity, and professionalism and have a reputation as excellent and highly effective teachers.

The referral and placement assistance process includes guidance and counseling on alternative certification programs, certification requirements, and identification of potential employment opportunities. The most important part of this process is referral. Individuals in the TTT database will be referred to school districts requesting lists of TTT participants interested in teaching in their state. Additionally, information will be provided to participants regarding teacher shortages reported by school districts. Those servicemembers interested in becoming a teacher should contact their education center about submitting an application for TTT through DANTES. Servicemembers can obtain additional information about TTT by calling (800) 231-6242, writing to DANTES Troops-to-Teachers, 6490 Saufley Field Road, Pensacola, FL 32509-5243, or visiting the TTT website: *voled.doded.mil/dantes/ttt/index.htm.*

UNIQUE NONTRADITIONAL EDUCATIONAL OPPORTUNITIES

Some colleges and universities may grant college credit to servicemembers for national and professional certifications, Defense Language Institute (DLI) courses, and Defense Language Proficiency Tests (DLPTs).

National Certification Tests

A national certification test evaluates whether an individual has the specified degree of knowledge and skill required to earn certification as a professional in a particular field. National certifications are used in the civilian community to establish a common level of expertise within certain career fields. Servicemembers who pass national certification tests are recognized alongside their civilian counterparts as professionals in their respective fields.

College Credit for National Certification Tests

In addition to providing professional credentials, these tests are used by some nontraditional institutions, such as Excelsior College, as the basis for awarding college credit for life and work experience. DANTES has agreements with many professional agencies that allow their examinations to be administered at military education centers worldwide. Make an appointment and talk to your education officer about when you can take these tests. Test dates and availability, as well as costs, vary.

Types of National Certification Tests Offered

Many of the national certification tests are listed below:

American Association of Bioanalysts (AAB) Board of Registry
www.aab.org

American Board of General Dentistry (ABGD)
www.agd.org

American Board of Industrial Hygiene (ABIH) Board of Certified Safety Professionals (BCSP) Joint Committee for Certification of Occupational Health and Safety Technologist
www.bcsp.com/joint.html

American Council on Exercise (ACE)
www.acefitness.org

American Institute of Constructors (AIC)
www.constructorcertification.org

American Medical Technologists (AMT)
www.amt1.com

American Nurses Credentialing Center (ANCC)
www.nursingworld.org

American Society for Industrial Security (ASIS)
www.asisonline.org

American Society of Military Comptrollers (ASMC)
www.asmconline.org

American Society for Quality (ASQ)
www.asq.org
American Speech-Language-Hearing Association (ASHA)
www.asha.org
Association of Boards of Certification (ABC)
www.abccert.org
Association of State and Provincial Psychology Boards (ASPPB)
www.asppb.org
Board of Certification for Emergency Nursing (BCEN)
www.ena.org
Board of Certified Safety Professionals (BCSP)
www.bcsp.com/joint.html
Cardiovascular Credentialing International (CCI)
www.cci-online.org
Certified Technical Trainer (CTT)
www.chauncey.com
Dental Assisting National Board (DANB)
www.dentalassisting.com
Education Institute of the American Hotel/Motel Association
(EIAH&MA) *www.ei-ahma.org*
Electronics Technician Association International (ETA-I)
www.eta-sda.com
Institute for Certification of Computing Professionals (ICCP)
www.iccp.org
Institute of Certified Professional Managers (ICPM)
cob.jmu.edu/icpm
Institute for Personal Finance (IPF)
www.afcpe.org
International Association of Administrative Professionals (IAAP)
www.iaap-hq.org
International Food Service Executives Association (IFSEA)
www.ifsea.org
Liaison Council on Certification for the Surgical Technologist
(LCC-ST) *www.lcc-st.org*
National Association of Radio and Telecommunications Engineers,
Inc. (NARTE) *www.narte.org*
National Association of Social Workers (NASW)
www.socialworkers.org

National Board for the Certification of Orthopaedic Technologist
(NBCOT) *www.nbcot.org*

National Board of Respiratory Care (NBRC)
www.nbrc.org

National Commission for the Certification of Crane Operators
(NCCCO) *www.nccco.org*

National Environmental Health Association (NEHA)
www.neha.org

National Institute for Automotive Service Excellence (ASE)
www.asecert.org

National Institute for the Certification in Engineering Technology
(NICET) *www.nicet.org*

National Institute for the Certification of Healthcare Sterile Processing
and Distribution Personnel (NICHSPDP)
www.sterileprocessing.org

National Registry of Emergency Medical Technicians (NREMT)
www.nremt.org

National Strength and Conditioning Association (NSCA)
www.nsca-cc.org

Society of Broadcast Engineers (SBE)
www.sbe.org

Defense Language Institute Courses

The Defense Language Institute (DLI) at the Presidio of Monterey, California, teaches a variety of foreign languages to military and U.S. government personnel. Languages taught at the DLI include modern European languages, Arabic, Chinese, Japanese, Russian, and Tagalog.

College Credit for DLI Courses

All DLI courses have been evaluated by ACE and are recommended for varying amounts of college credit. The courses at DLI normally last between six and eighteen months. Longer courses are generally recommended for more college credit than shorter courses. Even the short courses, however, can be valuable sources of college credit. For example, the basic Spanish course lasts six months (twenty-five weeks) and is recommended by ACE for 12 semester hours of college credit in the following categories: 3 semester hours in Spanish Elements I, 3 semester hours in Spanish Elements II, 3 semester hours in Spanish Composition and Culture, and 3 semester hours in Spanish Readings.

Getting a Transcript From DLI

Servicemembers who have completed a course at DLI may request a transcript by sending a written request to DLI/FLC, Academic Records Division, Presidio of Monterey, CA 93944-5006. Include your full name, social security number, course number (if known), course name, dates of attendance, and the address to where you would like the transcript sent.

The DLI transcript is free.

DLI Accreditation

The Defense Language Institute is accredited by the Accrediting Commission for Community and Junior Colleges of the Western Association of Schools and Colleges.

For more information about DLI, contact your military career counselor or visit the DLI website: *dli-www.army.mil.*

Defense Language Proficiency Tests

Defense Language Proficiency Tests (DLPTs) measure the ability to speak, read, and understand a language. The DLPT is related to the Defense Language Institute, but only in some ways. When students complete language courses at DLI, they are required to take the DLPT to measure their speaking, listening, and reading abilities. The DLPT is also used as the basis for awarding foreign language proficiency pay (FLPP) to servicemembers in select fields. The DLPT is free.

The DLPT is not restricted to DLI graduates. Anyone who believes that he or she has proficiency in a foreign language may request to take a DLPT. This does not mean that everyone who requests to take the DLPT is allowed to do so. Factors that are considered when approving the request include the commander's recommendation, the justification for taking the test, military specialty requirements, and the service's need for the language. Each service has its own process for requesting the DLPT.

College Credit for a DLPT

Some nontraditional schools, such as Excelsior College, award college credit for certain scores on the DLPT. There is an important distinction between DLI courses and the DLPT. Basic courses completed at DLI are normally only recommended for lower-level baccalaureate degree credit. Certain scores on the DLPT result in recommended college credit in both lower and upper divisions. The DLPT can be a valuable source of upper-level college credit for servicemembers seeking a bachelor's degree. Much of the credit awarded on the DLPT is in addition to any credit already received from DLI courses. For a DLPT score to be considered official, it must be annotated on an official test form, such as DA Form 330, *Language Proficiency Questionnaire,* and signed by the reporting officer (normally the test proctor). For the purposes of awarding college credit, most schools require a certified copy of the official DLPT scores.

Getting a Certified Copy of DLPT Results

A certified copy may be obtained from the test control officer, who normally administers the DLPT in your area, or from your education officer. In some cases, the personnel officer in charge (OIC) or noncommissioned OIC (NCOIC) may agree to certify a copy of your DLPT results, as long as an original copy is on file in your personnel records. If you need a certified copy of a DLPT taken at the DLI, you can request in writing that a certified copy be sent to you or the school you are attending. All requests for DLPTs should be sent to DLI/FLC, Attn: EST, DLPT Score Reports, Presidio of Monterey, CA 93944-5006. Be sure to include your full name, social security number, the language tested, the date you took the DLPT, and the address of the school where you want the copy sent. Request that the DLPT copy be certified. Most schools will not accept DLPT copies, certified or not, that are mailed by the student; the certifying official must mail the DLPT for you.

18

Fraudulent Schools: The Importance of Accreditation

It is important that any school you use be fully accredited by one of the accrediting agencies mentioned in this book. Fraudulent schools and phony degrees should be avoided at all costs. Fraudulent schools, often called "diploma mills," are business schemes designed to make money by selling fake degrees. The unscrupulous con men and women who set up and operate these "schools" will often sell any degree, including a medical degree, to anyone.

DIPLOMA MILLS
Buying a degree from a diploma mill is like buying a fake driver's license. Eventually, someone will notice and you will get caught. Most employers, including the armed forces, check to ensure that degrees are obtained from legitimate institutions of higher learning. Even though it is sometimes technically legal to buy a phony degree, it is unethical and usually against the law to use a phony degree to obtain a government job or a promotion. Most employers, including the military, have strict rules about the legitimacy and acceptance of degrees. The bottom line is that using a degree purchased from a diploma mill can lead to embarrassment and prosecution and can cause you to lose money, time, a job, a promotion, and the respect of your friends, family, and coworkers.

The Difference between Diploma Mills and Nontraditional Schools
This book is full of reputable schools that offer legitimate nontraditional shortcuts to help servicemembers pursue a college degree. The primary dif-

ference between reputable and fraudulent schools is accreditation. Reputable schools are accredited by recognized accrediting agencies, and diploma mills are not.

Another difference is the work required to complete a degree. Legitimate schools may offer nontraditional programs or shortcuts, but they do require work or proof of prior learning. Diploma mills will award a degree on the basis of "life experience" alone and require only a check, credit card, or money order. There are legitimate situations where credit for life experience may be granted, but no reputable school will offer a degree solely on the basis of life experience without proof of prior learning. A common e-mail advertisement circulating for a diploma mill service reads:

> UNIVERSITY DIPLOMAS: Obtain a prosperous future, money-earning power, and the admiration of all. Diplomas from prestigious nonaccredited universities based on your present knowledge and life experience. No required tests, classes, books, or interviews. Bachelor's, master's, MBA, and doctorate (Ph.D.) diplomas available in the field of your choice. No one is turned down. Confidentiality assured. CALL NOW to receive your diploma within days!!! (123) 456-7890. Call 24 hours a day, 7 days a week, including Sundays and holidays.

Besides junk e-mail, these schools may have impressive websites and advertise in newspapers and magazines. Unfortunately, it is common to see advertisements for diploma mills in the classified sections of some national magazines and newspapers. Regardless of what their literature may say, the proprietors of diploma mills make money by preying on unsuspecting students wanting to pursue a degree by the quickest and easiest means possible.

Remember, the primary difference between reputable and fraudulent schools is accreditation. Servicemembers should always verify a school's accreditation before applying, before reading about their degree programs, and especially before sending any money.

ACCREDITATION

Accreditation means that a school has been evaluated and approved by an accrediting agency or association found by the U.S. Department of Education to be a reliable authority regarding the quality of education offered by educational institutions or programs. The Department of Education categorizes accrediting agencies and associations as either regional institutional accrediting associations or national institutional and specialized accrediting agencies.

Accreditation is very important, because if you attend a school that is not accredited by a U.S. accrediting agency, you may be wasting both your time and your money. Many employers, both civilian and government, do not recognize degrees granted by institutions that are not accredited by an agency or association approved by the U.S. Department of Education. This also means that many accredited schools do not accept college credit transferred from nonaccredited schools. An institution must be accredited before most federal and private financial assistance can be granted.

If a School Claims That It Is Accredited, Can You Believe It?

You cannot always believe what you read in a college brochure or catalog. Many schools claim that they are accredited by this or that world organization or agency. There are many accrediting organizations that are not recognized by the U.S. Department of Education as being reliable authorities on the quality of education. Many of these organizations have poor reputations, and their approval or "accreditation" of a school means very little. Some diploma mills have even created their own accrediting organization just to accredit their own school. Of course, these phony accrediting organizations are not recognized by the Department of Education. Before enrolling and spending your money on a school, make sure that the school is accredited by an agency or organization approved by the U.S. Department of Education.

Verifying Accreditation

Servicemembers planning to enroll at an institution should contact the accrediting agency to verify that a school really is accredited. All regional institutional accrediting associations and national institutional and specialized accrediting agencies recognized by the U.S. Department of Education are listed below:

Regional Institutional Accrediting Agencies

Middle States Association of Colleges and Schools, Commission on
  Higher Education
3624 Market Street
Philadelphia, PA 19104
Phone: (215) 662-5606
Fax: (215) 662-5950
Web address: *www.msache.org*

New England Association of Schools and Colleges, Commission on
    Institutions of Higher Education
209 Burlington Road
Bedford, MA 01730-1433
Phone: (781) 271-0022
Fax: (781) 271-0950
Web address: *www.neasc.org*

New England Association of Schools and Colleges, Commission on
    Technical and Career Institutions
209 Burlington Road
Bedford, MA 01730-1433
Phone: (781) 271-0022
Fax: (781) 271-0950
Web address: *www.neasc.org*

North Central Association of Colleges and Schools, Executive Board
    of the Commission on Schools
Arizona State University
P.O. Box 873011
Tempe, AZ 85287-3011
Phone: (800) 525-9517
Fax: (602) 965-9423
Web address: *www.nca.asu.edu*

North Central Association of Colleges and Schools, The Higher
    Learning Commission
30 North LaSalle Street, Suite 2400
Chicago, IL 60602
Phone: (312) 263-0456 or (800) 621-7440
Fax: (312) 263-7462
Web address: *www.ncahigherlearningcommission.org*

Northwest Association of Schools and Colleges, Commission
    on Colleges
11130 NE 33rd Place, Suite 120
Bellevue, WA 98004
Phone: (425) 827-2005
Fax: (425) 827-3395
Web address: *www.cocnasc.org*

Southern Association of Colleges and Schools, Commission
on Colleges
1866 Southern Lane
Decatur, GA 30033-4097
Phone: (404) 679-4501 ext. 512 or (800) 248-7701
Fax: (404) 679-4558
Web address: *www.sacs.org*

Western Association of Schools and Colleges, Accrediting
Commission for Community and Junior Colleges
3402 Mendocino Avenue
Santa Rosa, CA 95403
Phone: (707) 569-9177
Fax: (707) 569-9179
Web address: *www.wascweb.org*

Western Association of Schools and Colleges, Accrediting
Commission for Schools
533 Airport Boulevard, Suite 200
Burlingame, CA 94010
Phone: (650) 696-1060
Fax: (650) 696-1867
Web address: *www.wascweb.org*

Western Association of Schools and Colleges, Accrediting
Commission for Senior Colleges and Universities
985 Atlantic Avenue, Suite 100
Alameda, CA 94501
Phone: (510) 748-9001
Fax: (510) 748-9797
Web address: *www.wascweb.org*

National Institutional and Specialized Accrediting Associations
Acupuncture and Oriental Medicine
Accreditation Commission for Acupuncture and Oriental Medicine
Phone: (301) 608-9680
Fax: (301) 608-9576

Allied Health
Accrediting Bureau of Health Education Schools
Phone: (703) 533-2082
Fax: (703) 533-2095
Web address: *www.abhes.org*

Art and Design
National Association of Schools of Art and Design, Commission on
    Accreditation
Phone: (703) 437-0700
Fax: (703) 437-6312
Web address: *www.arts-accredit.org*

Bible College Education
Accrediting Association of Bible Colleges, Commission on
    Accreditation
Phone: (407) 207-0808
Fax: (407) 207-0840
Web address: *www.aabc.org*

Business
Accrediting Council for Independent Colleges and Schools
Phone: (202) 336-6780
Fax: (202) 842-2593
Web address: *www.acics.org*

Chiropractic
The Council on Chiropractic Education, Commission on Accreditation
Phone: (480) 443-8877
Fax: (480) 483-7333
Web address: *www.cce-usa.org*

Christian Education
Transnational Association of Christian Colleges and Schools,
    Accrediting Commission
Phone: (804) 525-9539
Fax: (804) 525-9538
Web address: *www.tracs.org*

Clinical Laboratory Science
National Accrediting Agency for Clinical Laboratory Sciences
Phone: (773) 714-8880
Fax: (773) 714-8886
Web address: *www.naacles.org*

Continuing Education
Accrediting Council for Continuing Education and Training
Phone: (202) 955-1113
Fax: (202) 955-1118
Web address: *www.accet.org*

Cosmetology
National Accrediting Commission of Cosmetology Arts and Sciences
Phone: (703) 527-7600
Fax: (703) 527-8811
Web address: *www.naccas.org*

Dance
National Association of Schools of Dance, Commission on
    Accreditation
Phone: (703) 437-0700
Fax: (703) 437-6312
Web address: *www.arts-accredit.org*

Dental and Dental Auxiliary Programs
American Dental Association, Commission on Dental Accreditation
Phone: (312) 440-2500 or (800) 621-8099
Fax: (312) 440-2915
Web address: *www.ada.org*

Dietetics
The American Dietetic Association, Commission on Accreditation
    Dietetics Education
Phone: (312) 899-4872
Fax: (312) 899-4817
Web address: *www.eatright.org/caade*

Distance Education and Training
Distance Education and Training Council, Accrediting Commission
Phone: (202) 234-5100
Fax: (202) 332-1386
Web address: *www.detc.org*

Engineering
Accreditation Board for Engineering and Technology, Inc.
Phone: (410) 347-7700
Fax: (410) 625-2238
Web address: *www.abet.org*

Funeral Service Education
American Board of Funeral Service Education, Committee on
    Accreditation
Phone: (207) 878-6530
Fax: (207) 797-7686
Web address: *www.abfse.org*

Health Services Administration
Accrediting Commission on Education for Health Services
    Administration
Phone: (202) 638-5131
Fax: (202) 638-3429
Web address: *monkey.hmi.missouri.edu/acehsa/*

Journalism and Mass Communications
Accrediting Council on Education in Journalism and Mass
    Communications
Phone: (785) 864-3986
Fax: (785) 864-5225
Web address: *www.cc.ukans.edu/~acejmc/*

Law
American Bar Association, Council of the Section of Legal Education
    and Admissions to the Bar
Phone: (317) 264-8340
Fax: (317) 264-8355
Web address: *www.abanet.org/legaled/*

Liberal Education
American Academy for Liberal Education
Phone: (202) 452-8611
Fax: (202) 452-8620
Web address: *www.aale.org*

Marriage and Family Therapy
American Association for Marriage and Family Therapy, Commission
    on Accreditation for Marriage and Family Therapy Education
Phone: (202) 467-5111
Fax: (202) 232-2329
Web address: *www.aamft.org*

Medicine
Liaison Committee on Medical Education
Phone: (312) 464-4493
Fax: (312) 464-5830
Phone: (202) 828-0596
Fax: (202) 828-1125
Web address: *www.lcme.org*

Montessori Education
Montessori Accreditation Council for Teacher Education, Commission
    on Accreditation
Phone: (262) 595-3335 or (888) 446-2283
Fax: (262) 595-3332
Web address: *www.MACTE.org*

Music
National Association of Schools of Music, Commission on
    Accreditation, Commission on Non-Degree-Granting Accreditation,
    Commission on Community/Junior College Accreditation
Phone: (703) 437-0700
Fax: (703) 437-6312
Web address: *www.arts-accredit.org*

Naturopathy and Naturopathic Medicine
Council on Naturopathic Medical Education
Phone: (541) 687-7183
Web address: *www.cnme.org*

Nuclear Medicine Technology
Joint Review Committee on Educational Programs in Nuclear
    Medicine Technology
Phone: (406) 883-0003
Fax: (406) 883-0022
Web address: *www.jrcnmt.org*

Nurse Anesthesia
American Association of Nurse Anesthetists, Council on Accreditation
    of Nurse Anesthesia Educational Programs
Phone: (847) 692-7050
Fax: (847) 693-7137
Web address: *www.aane.com*

Nurse-Midwifery
American College of Nurse-Midwives, Division of Accreditation
Phone: (202) 728-9877
Fax: (202) 728-9897
Web address: *www.midwife.org*

Nurse Practitioners
National Association of Nurse Practitioners in Women's Health,
    Council on Accreditation
Phone: (202) 543-9693
Fax: (202) 543-9858
Web address: *www.npwh.org*

Nursing
Commission on Collegiate Nursing Education
Phone: (202) 887-6791
Fax: (202) 887-8476
Web address: *www.aacn.nche.edu/accreditation/index.htm*

National League for Nursing Accrediting Commission
Phone: (800) 669-1656
Fax: (212) 812-0390
Web address: *www.accrediting-comm-nlnac.org*

Occupational Education
Accrediting Commission of Career Schools and Colleges of
  Technology
Phone: (703) 247-4212
Fax: (703) 247-4533
Web address: *www.accsct.org*
Council on Occupational Education
Phone: (770) 396-3898 or (800) 917-2081
Fax: (770) 396-3790
Web address: *www.council.org*

Occupational Therapy
American Occupational Therapy Association, Accreditation Council
  for Occupational Therapy Education
Phone: (301) 652-2682
Fax: (301) 652-7711
Web address: *www.aota.org*

Opticianry
Commission on Opticianry Accreditation
Phone: (703) 941-9110
Web address: *www.coaccreditation.com*

Optometry
American Optometric Association, Council on Optometric Education
Phone: (314) 991-4100
Fax: (314) 991-4101

Osteopathic Medicine
American Osteopathic Association, Bureau of Professional Education
Phone: (312) 202-8000
Fax: (312) 202-8200/8202
Web address: *www.aoa-net-org*

Pastoral Education
Association for Clinical Pastoral Education, Inc., Accreditation
  Commission
Phone: (404) 320-1472
Fax: (404) 320-0849
Web address: *www.acpe.edu*

Pharmacy
American Council on Pharmaceutical Education
Phone: (312) 664-3575
Fax: (312) 664-4652
Web address: *www.acpe-accredit.org*

Physical Therapy
American Physical Therapy Association, Commission on Accreditation in Physical Therapy Education
Phone: (703) 706-3245
Fax: (703) 684-7343
Web address: *www.apta.org*

Podiatry
American Podiatric Medical Association, Council on Podiatric Medical Education
Phone: (301) 571-9200
Fax: (301) 581-9299
Web address: *www.apma.org*

Psychology
American Psychological Association, Committee on Accreditation
Phone: (202) 336-5979
Fax: (202) 336-5978
Web address: *www.apa.org/ed/accred.html*

Public Health
Council on Education for Public Health
Phone: (202) 789-1050
Fax: (202) 789-1895
Web address: *www.ceph.org*

Rabbinical and Talmudic Education
Association of Advanced Rabbinical and Talmudic Schools, Accreditation Commission
Phone: (212) 477-0950
Fax: (212) 533-5335

Radiologic Technology
Joint Review Committee on Education in Radiologic Technology
Phone: (312) 704-5300
Fax: (312) 704-5304
Web address: *www.jrcert.org*

Speech-Language Pathology and Audiology
American Speech-Language-Hearing Association, Council on Academic Accreditation
Phone: (301) 897-5700
Fax: (301) 571-0457
Web address: *www.asha.org*

Teacher Education
National Council for Accreditation of Teacher Education
Phone: (202) 466-7496
Fax: (202) 296-6620
Web address: *www.ncate.org*

Theater
National Association of Schools of Theatre, Commission on Accreditation
Phone: (703) 437-0700
Fax: (703) 437-6312
Web address: *www.arts-accredit.org*

Theology
Association of Theological Schools in the United States and Canada, Commission on Accrediting
Phone: (412) 788-6505
Fax: (412) 788-6510
Web address: *www.ats.edu*

Veterinary Medicine
American Veterinary Medical Association, Council on Education
Phone: (847) 925-8070 or (800) 248-2862
Fax: (847) 925-1329
Web address: *www.avma.org*

Other
New York State Board of Regents
Phone: (518) 474-5844
Fax (518) 473-4909
Web address: *www.nysed.gov*

19

Final Tips

Remember that education involves willpower and discipline as much as it does intellect. Getting started is often a large part of the battle, and by reading this book, you have already begun your educational journey. By now you should feel more comfortable, more optimistic, and more educated about your opportunities to pursue a college degree.

The following study and test-taking tips offer some practical advice. These tips have been gleaned from years of experience and tempered by both success and failure. They have already been proven effective by many servicemembers pursuing a college education. Use them, and your journey to college education will be an easier one.

STUDY TIPS

1. Study in a location free from distractions. If you need background noise to concentrate, it is better to use the radio than the television. Be sure to tune the radio to a classical station so that you won't be tempted to sing along with the music. Classical music also has a calming effect that facilitates concentration.
2. Develop a study routine by studying in the same place daily. Studying daily in shorter increments of time works much better than cramming the night before a test.
3. Reward yourself for positive study habits by saving dessert, rental movies, and enjoyable hobbies until after you have completed your daily studying. Be sure that your studying is focused on learning or mastering a particular concept or quantitative amount of knowledge rather than on the amount of time spent studying. In other words, focus on learning objectives rather than studying for a set amount of time.

4. Kill two birds with one stone by studying while you exercise. Treadmills and exercise bicycles allow for simultaneous reading and exercise. Also, public libraries and bookstores often have books on cassette or compact disk, which can be used in a portable cassette or CD player during exercise.

5. Review studied material as much as practical within the first twenty-four hours after studying. Most forgetting occurs during this period, so reinforcement and repetition are fundamental. By reviewing regularly, your retention of the studied material will improve markedly.

TEST-TAKING TIPS

1. Learn as much as possible about a test before you take it. Ask your education officer for any bulletins, sample tests, or flyers available on the test you will be taking. Learn what is expected, the exact type of test to be given, its format, what knowledge is being tested, and how the tests are scored. Knowing as much as possible about the test in advance will relieve stress and help you feel more comfortable during the test.

2. Prepare as much as possible. Take advantage of the sample tests offered by your education center, and practice taking the sample tests under timed conditions. Review any questions that you miss. Pay particular attention to the directions for each question missed. Many questions are answered incorrectly because the directions were not fully understood or not fully read.

3. Be mentally and physically alert. Get plenty of sleep the night before the test. Depart for the test site early as a precaution against unexpected delays, such as traffic. Take your identification and several no. 2 pencils. Dress comfortably. Select a seat in the testing room away from potential distractions. Do not sit next to your friends.

4. On mathematical questions, do not waste time completing long computations unless the question asks for a specific answer. If an approximate answer is required, eliminate the incorrect answers before finishing long computations.

APPENDICES

Appendix A

Abbreviations

AA	Associate of Arts degree
AARTS	Army/ACE Registry Transcript System
AAS	Associate of Applied Science degree
AASCU	American Association of State Colleges and Universities
ACAP	Army Career and Alumni Program
ACCP	Army Correspondence Course Program
ACE	American Council on Education
ACES	Army Continuing Education System
ACF	Army College Fund
ACT	American College Testing
ACT-PEP	American College Testing Proficiency Examination Program
AEC	Army Education Center
AFSC	Air Force Specialty Code
AIPD	Army Institute for Professional Development
AIT	Advanced individual training
AMU	American Military University
ANCOC	Army Advanced Noncommissioned Officer Course
AP	Advanced placement
AQ	Additional qualification
AQD	Navy additional qualification designation
AS	Associate of Science degree
ASI	Army additional skills identifier
ASVAB	Armed Services Vocational Aptitude Battery
AUAO	Army University Access Online
BA	Bachelor of Arts degree

BDFS	Bachelor's degree for soldiers
BNCOC	Army Basic Noncommissioned Officer Course
BS	Bachelor of Science degree
CAGIS	DANTES Computer Assisted Guidance Information Systems
CAI	Career Assessment Inventory
CCAF	Community College of the Air Force
CCE	Course credit by examination (Ohio University)
CEM	Air Force chief enlisted manager
CISS	Campbell Interest and Skill Survey
CLEP	College Level Examination Program
CONUS	Continental United States
CPB	Corporation for Public Broadcasting
CPP	Career Planning Program
CWO	Chief warrant officer
DANTES	Defense Activity for Non-Traditional Education Support
DETC	Distance Education and Training Council
DLI/FLC	Defense Language Institute/Foreign Language Center
DLPT	Defense Language Proficiency Test
DOE	Department of Education
DSST	DANTES Subject Standardized Test
ECE	Excelsior College Examination
ECI	Air Force Extension Course Institute
ESO	Education services officer
ETS	Educational testing service
FAST	Functional academic skills training
FRA	Fleet Reserve Association
GED	General Educational Development
GMAT	Graduate Management Admission Test
GPA	Grade point average
GRE	Graduate Record Examination
GT	General technical
ICCP	Institute for Certification of Computing Professionals
LDO	Navy limited duty officer
LMMS	Air Force leadership, management, and military studies
LSAT	Law School Admission Test
MA	Master of Arts degree
MASP	Military Academic Skills Program
MBTI	Myers-Briggs Type Indicator

MCSEN	Marine Corps Satellite Education Network
MGIB	Montgomery GI Bill
MILPO	Military personnel office
MOS	Military occupational specialty
MS	Master of Science degree
NCC	Navy College Center
NCLC	Navy College Learning Center
NCLP	Navy College Learning Program
NCOES	NCO Education System
NCP	Navy College Program
NCPACE	Navy College Program for Afloat College Education
NEC	Navy enlisted classification
NMCRS	Navy and Marine Corps Relief Society
NOBC	Navy officer billet classification
OCS	Officer candidate school
OSB	Officer selection battery
OTS	Air Force Officer Training School
PACE	Program for Afloat College Education
PLDC	Army Primary Leadership Development Course
PONSI	Program on Noncollegiate Sponsored Instruction
PPST	Pre-Professional Skills Test
QH	Quarter hour
RI	Air Force reporting identifier
ROTC	Reserve Officer Training Corps
SAT	Scholastic Aptitude Test
SDI	Air Force special duty identifier
SDS	Holland Self-Directed Search
SH	Semester hour
SI	Skills identifier
SMART	Sailor/Marine ACE Registry Transcript
SOC	Servicemembers Opportunity Colleges
SOCAD	SOC Army degrees
SOC	Associate Degree Program (now known as SOCAD-2)
SOCAD-2	SOC Army degrees (associate degree)
SOCAD-4	SOC Army degrees (bachelor's degree)
SOCBDFS	SOC bachelor's degree for soldiers (now known as SOCAD-4)
SOCMAR-2	SOC Marine Corps (associate degree)
SOCMAR-4	SOC Marine Corps (bachelor's degree)
SOCNAV-2	SOC Navy (associate degree)

SOCNAV-4	SOC Navy (bachelor's degree)
SQI	Army special qualifications identifier
SSI	Strong Interest Inventory
SSP	Navy subspecialty
TA	Tuition assistance
TABE	Test of Adult Basic Education
TAMP	Navy Transition Assistance Management Program
TCO	Test control officer
TDY	Temporary duty
TECEP	Thomas Edison College Examination Program
TESC	Thomas Edison State College
UIC	Unit identification code
USAFI	United States Air Force Institute
USMAP	United Services Military Apprenticeship Program
VA	Veterans Administration
VMET	Verification of Military Experience and Training

Appendix B

Glossary

Associate degree A degree that normally requires completion of at least two but less than four years of full-time equivalent college-level work (usually 60 semester hours).

Bachelor's degree A degree that normally requires completion of four but no more than five years of full-time equivalent college-level work (usually 120 semester hours).

Doctorate A degree that normally requires completion of a program of study beyond the master's degree. It is the highest degree that can be awarded for graduate study. Examples include the Doctor of Philosophy (Ph.D.) and the Doctor of Education (Ed.D.).

First professional degree A degree that requires completion of a program that includes at least two years of college-level work before entering the program, completion of the academic requirements to begin practice in the profession, and a total of at least six academic years of college-level work to complete the degree program, including prior required college-level work and the length of the professional program itself. Examples include the Degree in Law (J.D.) and the Degree in Medicine (M.D.).

Master's degree A degree that normally requires completion of a program of study, consisting of the full-time equivalent of one to two academic years of work beyond the bachelor's degree.

Quarter A unit of time of an academic calendar. The quarter system is used less often than the semester system. Colleges using the quarter system normally divide the school year into three quarters, with the first quarter lasting from September to December, the second quarter from January to March, and the third quarter from March to May. The fourth quarter constitutes summer vacation.

Quarter hour A unit of college credit used to represent completion of a subject normally pursued for a period of approximately one hour per week during the quarter. This unit of college credit is used less often than the semester hour. Most colleges using the quarter system offer classes in units of 3 quarter hours. A class worth 3 quarter hours, for example, would meet for approximately 3 hours during each week of the quarter.

Semester The most common unit of time of an academic calendar. Normally, a school year is divided into two semesters, with the first semester lasting from August to December, and the second semester from January to May.

Semester hour A unit of college credit used to represent completion of a subject normally pursued for a period of approximately one hour per week for the semester. This is the most common unit of college credit. Most college classes are offered in units of 3 semester hours, although classes worth more or less credit are not uncommon. A class worth 3 semester hours would meet for approximately three hours during each week of the semester.

Appendix C

Major Military Education Centers

Azores
Air Force Education Office
  Lajes Field

Bahrain
Navy College Office
  NSA Bahrain

Belgium
Army Education Center
  Shape

Bosnia
Army Education Center
  Tuzla
  Camp Dobol
  Camp McGovern
  Camp Comanche
  Camp Butmir, Sarajevo

Cuba
Navy College Office
  Naval Station Guantanamo

Diego Garcia
Navy College Office
  NSF Diego Garcia

Egypt
Army Education Center
  MFO Sinai

Germany
Air Force Education Office
  Geilenkirchen Air Base
  Ramstein Air Base
  Spangdahlem Air Base
Army Education Center
  Ansbach-Katterbach
  Babenhausen
  Bad Kreuznach, Rose
    Barracks
  Bamberg, Warner Barracks
  Baumholder, Smith Barracks
  Buedingen, Armstrong
    Barracks
  Darmstadt, Cambrai-Fritsch
  Dexheim, Anderson
    Barracks
  Friedberg, Ray Barracks
  Giessen Army Depot
  Heidelberg, Patton Barracks
  Hohenfels
  Illesheim, Storck Barracks

Kaiserslautern, Kleber
  Kaserne
Mannheim, Coleman
  Barracks
Mannheim, Sullivan
  Barracks
Rhine Ordnance Barracks
Schweinfurt, Conn Barracks
Schweinfurt, Ledward
  Barracks
Schwetzingen, Tompkins
  Barracks
Stuttgart, Panzer Kaserne
Wiesbaden
Giebelstadt
Vilseck
Wuerzburg, Larson Barracks
Wuerzburg, Leighton
  Barracks

Greece
Navy College Office
  Souda Bay

Guam
Air Force Education Office
  Anderson Air Force Base
Navy College Office
  Naval Station Guam

Honduras
Army Education Center
  Soto Cano Air Base

Iceland
Air Force Education Office
  Keflavik Air Base
Navy College Office
  NAF Keflavik

Italy
Air Force Education Office
  Aviano Air Base
  Ghedi Air Base
Army Education Center
  Vicenza
Navy College Office
  NSA Lamaddalena
  NSA Naples
  Naval Air Station Sigonella

Japan
Air Force Education Office
  Misawa Air Base
  Yokota Air Base
Army Education Center
  Camp Zama
Navy College Office
  Naval Air Station Atsugi
  NFA Sasebo
  Naval Station Yokosuka
Marine Lifelong Learning
  Iwakuni MCAS

Japan (Okinawa)
Air Force Education Office
  Kadena Air Base
Army Education Center
  Torii Station
Marine Lifelong Learning
  Camp Butler
  Camp Courtney
  Camp Foster
  Camp Hansen
  Camp Kinser
  Camp Schwab
  Futenma MCAS
Navy College Office
  NAF Kadena

Korea
Air Force Education Office
  Kunsan Airbase
  Osan Airbase
Army Education Centers
  Camp Carroll
  Camp Casey
  Camp Garry Owen
  Camp Greaves
  Camp Henry
  Camp Hialeah
  Camp Hovey
  Camp Howze
  Camp Humphries
  Camp Long Eagle
  Camp Page
  Camp Red Cloud
  Camp Stanley

Kosovo
Army Education Center
  Camp Bondsteel

Kuwait
Army Education Center
  Camp Doha

Macedonia
Army Education Center
  Camp Able Sentry

Netherlands
Army Education Center
  Treebeek

Norway
Air Force Education Office
  Stravanger

Puerto Rico
Army Education Center
  Fort Buchanan
Navy College Office
  Roosevelt Roads

Saudi Arabia
Army Education Center
  Riyadh

Spain
Navy College Office
  Naval Station Rota

Turkey
Air Force Education Office
  Incirlik Airbase
  Izmir Airbase
Army Education Center
  Ankara

United Kingdom
Air Force Education Office
  Alconbury RAF Molesworth
  RAF Croughton
  RAF Lakenheath
  RAF Mildenhall
Army Education Center
  Menwith Hill Station
Navy College Office
  London

Alabama
Air Force Education Office
  Maxwell Air Force Base
Army Education Center
  Fort Rucker
  Redstone Arsenal

Alaska
Air Force Education Office
  Eielson Air Force Base
  Elmendorf Air Force Base
Army Education Center
  Fort Greely
  Fort Richardson
  Fort Wainwright

Arizona
Air Force Education Office
  Davis Monthan Air Force
    Base
  Luke Air Force Base
Army Education Center
  Fort Huachuca
  Yuma Proving Ground
Marine Lifelong Learning
  MCAS Yuma

Arkansas
Air Force Education Office
  Little Rock Air Force Base

California
Air Force Education Office
  Beale Air Force Base
  Edwards Air Force Base
  Los Angeles Air Force Base
  McClellan Air Force Base
  Travis Air Force Base
  Vandenberg Air Force Base
Army Education Center
  Fort Irwin
  Presidio of Monterey
Marine Lifelong Learning
  Barstow
  Camp Pendleton
  MCAS Miramar

Marine Corps Recruit Depot
  San Diego
  San Diego
  Twentynine Palms
Navy College Office
  NAWS China Lake
  NAB Coronado
  NAS Lemoore
  NAS North Island
  Naval Brig Miramar
  Naval Base Point Mugu
  NSA Port Hueneme
  NSA San Diego
  Naval Station San Diego
  Naval Submarine Base, San
    Diego
  NARCEN San Jose

Colorado
Air Force Education Office
  Peterson Air Force Base
Army Education Center
  Fort Carson

Connecticut
Navy College Office
  Submarine Base New
    London

Delaware
Air Force Education Office
  Dover Air Force Base

District Of Columbia
Air Force Education Office
  Bolling Air Force Base
Army Education Center
  Pentagon
  Walter Reed Army Medical
    Center

Navy College Office
NAVSTA Washington

Florida
Air Force Education Office
Eglin Air Force Base
Hurlburt Field
MacDill Air Force Base
Patrick Air Force Base
Tyndall Air Force Base
Army Education Center
Hq., U.S. Southern
Command, Miami
Navy College Office
NAS Jacksonville
NAS Key West
Naval Station Mayport

Georgia
Air Force Education Office
Moody Air Force Base
Robins Air Force Base
Army Education Center
Fort Benning
Fort Stewart
Hunter Army Airfield
Marine Lifelong Learning
Marine Corps Logistics Base
Albany
Navy College Office
Submarine Base Kings Bay

Hawaii
Air Force Education Office
Hickam Air Force Base
Army Education Center
Fort Shafter
Schofield Barracks
Tripler Army Medical Center

Marine Lifelong Learning
Camp H. M. Smith
Marine Corps Base Kaneohe
Bay
Navy College Office
Naval Station Pearl Harbor
NAVCOMSTA Wahiawawa

Idaho
Air Force Education Office
Mountain Home Air Force
Base

Illinois
Air Force Education Office
Scott Air Force Base
Navy College Office
Naval Training Center Great
Lakes

Kansas
Air Force Education Office
McConnell Air Force Base
Army Education Center
Fort Leavenworth
Fort Riley

Kentucky
Army Education Center
Fort Campbell
Fort Knox

Louisiana
Air Force Education Office
Barksdale Air Force Base
Army Education Center
Fort Polk
Navy College Office
NSA New Orleans

Maine
Navy College Office
  NAS Brunswick

Maryland
Air Force Education Office
  Andrews Air Force Base
Army Education Center
  Aberdeen Proving Grounds
  Fort Detrick
  Fort Meade
Navy College Office
  NAS Patuxent River
  NMC Bethesda

Massachusetts
Air Force Education Office
  Hanscom Air Force Base
Army Education Center
  Fort Devens

Mississippi
Air Force Education Office
  Columbus Air Force Base
  Keesler Air Force Base
Navy College Office
  Naval Air Station Meridian
  Naval Support Activity
    Gulfport
  NAVSTA Pascagoula

Missouri
Air Force Education Office
  Whiteman Air Force Base
Army Education Center
  Fort Leonard Wood
Marine Lifelong Learning
  MCSA Kansas City

Montana
Air Force Education Office
  Malmstrom Air Force Base

Nebraska
Air Force Education Office
  Offutt Air Force Base

New Jersey
Air Force Education Office
  McGuire Air Force Base
Army Education Center
  Fort Dix
  Fort Monmouth
Navy College Office
  Naval Station–Earle
  Naval Station–Lakehurst

New Mexico
Air Force Education Office
  Cannon Air Force Base
  Holloman Air Force Base
  Kirtland Air Force Base
Army Education Center
  White Sands Missile Range

Nevada
Air Force Education Office
  Nellis Air Force Base
Navy College Office
  NAS Fallon

New York
Army Education Center
  Fort Drum
  Fort Hamilton
  U.S. Military Academy West
    Point
Navy College Office
  Naval Training Unit–
    Ballston

North Carolina
Air Force Education Office
  Pope Air Force Base
  Seymour Johnson Air Force
    Base
Army Education Center
  Fort Bragg
Marine Lifelong Learning
  Camp Lejeune
  MCAS Cherry Point
  MCAS Jacksonville

North Dakota
Air Force Education Office
  Grand Forks Air Force Base
  Minot Air Force Base

Ohio
Air Force Education Office
  Wright Patterson Air Force
    Base

Oklahoma
Air Force Education Office
  Altus Air Force Base
  Tinker Air Force Base
  Vance Air Force Base
Army Education Center
  Fort Sill

Pennsylvania
Army Education Center
  Carlisle Barracks

Rhode Island
Navy College Office
  Naval Station Newport

South Carolina
Air Force Education Office
  Charleston Air Force Base
  Shaw Air Force Base
Army Education Center
  Fort Jackson
Marine Lifelong Learning
  Marine Corps Recruit Depot
    Parris Island
  MCAS Beaufort
Navy College Office
  Naval Station Charleston

South Dakota
Air Force Education Office
  Ellsworth Air Force Base

Tennessee
Air Force Education Office
  Arnold Air Force Base
Navy College Office
  NAS Millington

Texas
Air Force Education Office
  Brooks Air Force Base
  Dyess Air Force Base
  Goodfellow Air Force Base
  Kelly Air Force Base
  Lackland Air Force Base
  Laughlin Air Force Base
  Randolph Air Force Base
  Sheppard Air Force Base
Army Education Center
  Fort Bliss
  Fort Hood
  Fort Sam Houston
Navy College Office
  NAS Corpus Christi
  NAS Kingsville
  Naval Station Ingleside

Utah
Air Force Education Office
  Hill Air Force Base
Army Education Center
  Dugway Proving Grounds

Virginia
Air Force Education Office
  Langley Air Force Base
Army Education Center
  Fort Belvoir
  Fort Eustis
  Fort Lee
  Fort Monroe
  Fort Myer
Marine Lifelong Learning
  Henderson Hall
  Marine Corps Base Quantico
Navy College Office
  NAS Oceana
  Naval Air Base Little Creek
  Naval Medical Center
    Portsmouth
  Naval Station Norfolk

Washington
Air Force Education Office
  Fairchild Air Force Base
  McChord Air Force Base
Army Education Center
  Fort Lewis
Navy College Office
  NAS Whidbey Island
  Naval Station Everett
  Naval Station Puget Sound
  NSB Bangor

Wyoming
Air Force Education Office
  Warren Air Force Base

About the Author

Larry Anderson was born in Gallatin, Tennessee, in 1968 and joined the U.S. Army in 1987. He used many of the nontraditional methods he writes about to complete his own bachelor's and master's degrees while serving on active duty in the military. He left the Army as a sergeant first class in 2000 and now works for the Department of Defense as a civilian analyst. He authored the *Soldiers' Guide to a College Degree,* first edition, and expanded the scope to include all service college programs in this revised and retitled second edition.

Index

STACKPOLE BOOKS

Military Professional Reference Library

Armed Forces Guide to Personal Financial Planning
Air Force Officer's Guide
Airman's Guide
Army Officer's Guide
Army Dictionary and Desk Reference
Career Progression Guide
Combat Service Support Guide
Combat Leader's Field Guide
Enlisted Soldier's Guide
Guide to Effective Military Writing
Guide to Military Operations Other Than War
Job Search: Marketing Your Military Experience
Military Money Guide
NCO Guide
Reservist's Money Guide
Serviceman's Legal Guide
Servicemember's Guide to a College Degree
Today's Military Wife
Veteran's Guide to Benefits
Virtual Combat: A Guide to Distributed Interactive Simulation

Professional Reading Library

Beyond Terror
by Ralph Peters

Roots of Strategy: Books 1, 2, 3, and 4

Guardians of the Republic: A History of the NCO
by Ernest F. Fisher

Stackpole Books are available at your Exchange Bookstore or
Military Clothing Sales Store, or from Stackpole at
www.stackpolebooks.com *or* **1-800-732-3669**